Bake Yourself Happy

Steph Blackwell

Bake Yourself Happy

50 recipes to bring you joy

greenfinch

Contents

Introduction

I'm not sure where to start. Maybe with a thank you, for picking up this book, even if you immediately put it down again. There are thousands of fabulous books out there, so I'm incredibly grateful to you for casting even one eye over my musings.

For those who don't know me, I'm Steph and I love baking. I spend most of my days in the kitchen causing chaos with flour, butter, sugar, eggs and various other ingredients. I will warn you now, if you too find a passion for baking (which I hope you do), your kitchen will take on new characteristics – namely serious stickiness, a constant light dusting of flour and the occasional splatter of unidentifiable ingredients across the walls.

I was initially drawn to baking for its healing powers. I have struggled with my mental health since I was 17, and, much as I don't like to let it define me, it is a part of who I am. As such, finding ways to manage it is important. Where some people use knitting, pottery or yoga to find their Zen, I bake. It helps me feel more in control, it releases tension and it improves my concentration, focusing my butterfly brain. When it goes right, it's the most rewarding endeavour, and when it doesn't, at least I'll be concentrating on a different stress to the one I started with. Baking unleashes my creative side, too – one I didn't think I had. I've gained friends, and sharing kindness and love through the simple medium of baked goods yields unequivocal happiness for all involved – surely the ultimate goal in life?

Back in 2019, when I was still very much a novice at baking, I (somehow) managed to secure a place on *The Great British Bake Off*. It was a dream to be chosen, and the success I went on to achieve by reaching the final was beyond imaginable. I'm not going to lie, putting yourself forward for the nation's biggest baking show isn't exactly meditative. However, the experience was life-changing and my appearance on the show has afforded me incredible opportunities like this one – writing about the two things that I'm passionate about: baking and happiness.

My aim with this book is to enlighten you to the magic of baking: to help you experience a sense of achievement when rewarded with a tasty outcome, to encourage you to rekindle your inner child and creativity, to enhance your practical baking knowledge and above all improve your sense of well-being. I've also tried to provide as many tips as possible. Unfortunately, as with all good things, occasionally bakes just don't quite turn out how you expect them to – often it's simply bad luck and, actually, your greatest lessons are learned from your biggest mistakes, so there is no failure in my eyes. However, I've done my best to limit the likelihood of major catastrophe by providing all the tips and tricks that I've got up my sleeve.

Included in these pages are a few of my favourite creations; those that provide the ultimate calm, satisfaction and joy, be it through improving confidence, releasing tension or boosting mood. Some bakes are speedy, foolproof and rustic, while others require a bit more time, concentration and finesse. This book may not revolutionize your life, and, unfortunately, there is no guarantee that you will become a top pastry chef overnight, but I do hope it can shine a little light on your life in even the smallest way.

How Baking Brings Me Joy

For me, baking has been extremely therapeautic. Throughout my adult life, I've experienced bouts of debilitating depression, an eating disorder, obsessive tendencies and more recently, severe anxiety. Over time, I have learned to accept that it is part of my make-up. My brain is just wired in a slightly different way to others; sometimes the light switch isn't quite working properly, or the circuit becomes overloaded, and I lose power. I then seek some form of control and am prone to employing destructive behaviours. Understanding this has really helped me to be kinder to myself when things get difficult; it doesn't necessarily resolve the initial trigger, nor does it completely negate my instinct to spiral into a black hole of negativity and anxiety, but it does prompt me to engage in some positive activities, which can work almost like a crutch, as I wait for my brain to recover. I've tried various forms of therapy over the years, but the activity that revolutionized things for me was baking. I watched YouTube videos and *The Great British Bake Off* series on repeat until I knew all the words, then I decided I would have a go – and the rest is history. It's the thing I always turn to when I feel out of control – it provides comfort; it makes sense of time and gives me purpose; it engages all of my senses and encourages me to focus when my thoughts feel somewhat scattered; it encourages me to connect with others and gives me a boost of confidence when I am being hard on myself.

I often feel quite different to others, but when it comes to people seeking solace in baking, it would appear that I'm in good company. Queen of baking Mary Berry once stated in an interview with the *Guardian* that 'baking is physical and mental therapy'; meanwhile, culinary goddess Nigella Lawson marvels at how uplifting and comforting just mixing up a cake, rolling out biscuits or having her hands in dough can be. Similarly, friends of mine in the industry and many of the contestants who have stepped foot into the *Bake Off* tent recount tales of experiencing joy, comfort and mental relief through baking at some point in their life. This psychological advantage isn't limited to those living with mental health conditions; all can benefit from the joy of a humble 'quick-bake' cookie, the miracle of transforming basic ingredients into something truly delectable, the opportunity to unleash our inner creativity or the chance to truly unwind with a slow methodical bake.

Unsurprisingly, the tragedy, fear and isolation caused by the COVID-19 pandemic has taken its toll on our mental health. Almost instinctively, we started to engage in leisure activities to deal with the fear and feelings of restriction – they provided purpose, comfort and encouraged socialization, albeit virtual. One of the activities that really gripped people during that time was baking. Of course, the extent of the psychological burden sometimes goes beyond this simple fix, but I find it truly remarkable that something as simple as mixing a few ingredients and bunging them in the oven can nourish the mind, body and soul, and have such a profound effect on so many of us.

Baking can provide both short-term therapeutic advantages – momentary happiness, pleasure, relaxation, socialization and sensory stimulus – as well as long-term and enduring psychological benefits, such as acquiring knowledge or skills, self-actualization, self-enrichment, feelings of accomplishment and belonging, identity building, teaching coping mechanisms and offering career opportunities. Delving into a little more detail, researchers have established several specific ways in which baking can improve our mental health. These include:

Baking as a form of mindfulness and meditation

Mindfulness and meditation have become well established as useful techniques for reducing physical and mental stress, letting go of negativity and forcing us to approach life at a slower pace. Baking encourages us to concentrate as we weigh and measure ingredients, it engages all our senses, and we must stay present in the moment of creativity.

Baking for stress relief

Baking is a form of stress relief as it provides escapism from a destructive inner narrative. It is the perfect antidote to our tendency to rush, stress and fuss over things.

Baking for others as a form of altruism

Baking for others, either as a gift, celebration or as part of your career, is hugely rewarding. Quite simply, it makes us happy seeing others happy. Developing a recipe and creating a baked masterpiece with the intention of sharing it with others is seen as a form of altruism: a sacrifice made with love and good intention to nurture others.

Baking as a means for communication

Often people who struggle with their mental health will experience episodes of social withdrawal. Even when we know that seeing others will most probably alleviate feelings of hopelessness or sadness, we feel paralyzed and unable to engage. Baking represents a simple medium for us to reconnect

with people – initially we may only be capable of throwing a baked good over the threshold of our neighbour's front door, but over time, we may engage more with loved ones and friends, using the baked goods as a comfort blanket that enables us to communicate.

Baking to gain some control over our lives

The precision and scientific element involved in baking can be hugely advantageous. It can provide a useful coping mechanism, helping us exert some control over our surroundings. An understanding of the science gives us a grasp of the nutritional value of the food we are consuming, too, so foods are no longer labelled as 'good' and 'bad', 'healthy' or 'unhealthy', but nourishing.

Baking to promote self-expression

There is a positive correlation between creativity and improved well-being. Baking provides a wonderful outlet for creative expression; when it comes to art and creativity, there are no rules and there is no judgement of what is right or wrong. From flavour combinations to decorative flourishes, it's a way of setting free a portion of ourselves that has been locked away by our anxious minds.

Baking as a way to increase self-confidence

Typically, people who suffer with mental health conditions will experience feelings of low self-esteem. They will be overly self-critical and hold themselves up to unrealistic standards of perfection – I'm guilty of this. Baking can help overcome these negative thought patterns, providing fulfilment and giving us a sense of identity. It can make sense of our lives, make us feel worthwhile and ultimately help us to recognize our potential.

Despite the overwhelming evidence to suggest that baking can improve mental health, I think it's important to also recognize that we are all very different. Where one person finds freedom through music or reading, others may prosper in adrenaline-fuelled environments, with animals or outdoors. Baking may not be for everyone, and no one should feel a failure if it's not for them. I would argue that most love affairs take some time and commitment, so it's worth giving it a few goes, but if it doesn't light your spark, there are so many other wonderful resources that we can engage in to reap similar psychological rewards. Fundamentally, anything that helps us to feel more alive is worth our time.

In a world that falsely sells perfection as a standard we should aspire to, I hope that the messiness and somewhat primal nature of baking can help you to realize that average, OK, good, and even 'oops', are all we need to aim for. With baking you can make tons of mistakes, but it usually tastes great, and you can be sure that next time it will most likely be better. I hope that some of the recipes in this book can help you find a little pleasure, be it through distraction, peace, creativity or simply because it tastes good.

Ten Top Tips for Joyful Baking

1. **Get messy:** allow yourself the freedom to drop a bit of mixture on the floor, cover the surfaces in flour and liberally smear chocolate down the front of your apron. Baking doesn't have to be tidy or neat, your cake can be wonky and the icing uneven – it will still taste delicious.

2. **Don't set deadlines:** baking can sometimes feel like a chore if we pit ourselves against the clock. Allow yourself plenty of time to make your bakes – in many instances, recipes can be approached piecemeal across a couple of days, so give yourself a weekend to unwind with a slow and steady baking venture.

3. **Get creative:** baking is a science and – to a major extent – instructions must be followed to achieve the desired outcome. However, as I indicate in many of the recipes, you can make substitutions to suit the season or your tastes and needs. Likewise, decorate things with your own flair, don't be constrained by the accompanying photos or perfect images you see on social media.

4. **Bake at times that suit you:** my favourite time to bake is first thing in the morning, when I wake up and step into the kitchen like a little elf. I feel most peaceful, productive and calm at this time of day; it's my moment of Zen before the rest of the world wakes up. This time may not work for you, but find the time that does and aim to do most of your baking then for optimal happiness gains.

5. **Establish your happiest environment for baking:** for me it's alone, with my own thoughts, but you may prefer music, the TV or a podcast for company, or a friend to bake with.

6. **Don't bake tired:** if you're tired, approach baking with caution. I have rarely produced a good bake under the influence of too few Zs... funnily enough, I still continue to make this mistake, but take it from me, tiredness and baking don't complement each other.

7. **Get organized:** prepare all your ingredients and equipment before barrelling into a bake. In the culinary industry this is referred to as mise en place. On the odd occasion that I engage my brain and get everything organized in advance, my bakes are better, my enjoyment is greater and my kitchen remains significantly cleaner and tidier as a result.

8. ***Make notes:*** be cautious when scaling ingredients up or down. Some recipes just don't work when the proportions are altered too drastically, while others can be fine if you adjust the baking time and sometimes temperature accordingly. Most importantly, however, be methodical about any changes you make. Make sure you write up the original recipe in a notebook, then adjust all the measurements accordingly, double-check them and then work from this. Please don't be impulsive like me and assume your maths (and concentration) is up to making the alterations as you go. Having completed a bake, you can then use your template and make minor tweaks going forward to suit your preferences. Don't forget, we are all unique, so this is your chance to get creative with ingredients.

9. ***Start with a clean slate:*** if you enter the kitchen and it already looks like a small food explosion has taken place, you can only expect things to get worse... ultimately, the worst aspect of baking is the washing up – add to this a backlog of prior washing up and that calming, stress-busting endeavour can lose its charm!

10. ***Finally, and most importantly, lick the bowl!*** If you're baking for someone else, you might need to use a spatula, but when bowls need to be cleaned, consider yourself the first stage in the dishwashing process.

Before You Get Started

While I don't want to make baking sound scary, it's not always straightforward. Below I have listed as many helpful recipe notes as I can to shield you from potential mishaps, but the list of possible baking issues is endless and sometimes you just have to learn the hard way! I still have plenty of lessons to learn through countless future mistakes, I'm sure.

Read the recipe (read it twice): before you set out on a bake, check you have the ingredients and equipment required, then get started!

Prepare yourself: it's a good idea to weigh everything out before you start so it's easier to combine all the right ingredients in the right order.

Attention to detail matters: I am very precise when it comes to measurements and timings, which can sometimes be unnecessary, but recipes do rely on a certain degree of accuracy to be successful.

Be cautious when making substitutions: always check online to see whether two ingredients can be used interchangeably without ill effect.

Temperature matters: there will be a reason that a recipe states a particular ingredient should be a certain temperature, for example cold or softened butter. Not following the instruction is likely to have an effect on the final bake.

When baking bread, proving times vary drastically based on countless factors: ambient temperature and humidity, fat, sugars, the freshness of your yeast and additional ingredients are just a few of the major players. Baking bread is a continuous learning curve – it will keep you on your toes, but the result is worth it.

Ingredients

As a rule of thumb, higher quality ingredients – specifically sustainably produced and locally sourced – yield a tastier outcome. While this is a something to keep in mind generally, there are a few ingredients that you should pay special attention to.

Butter: opt for butter with a minimum 82 per cent butterfat content as it will contain less water, resulting in bakes with a richer taste, softer texture and faster meltability.

Eggs: in some recipes I specifically state an amount of egg in grams. This is for accuracy and refers to the weight of egg once cracked from its shell – i.e. a large egg will yield around 55g (2¼oz) egg. The same applies to yolks and whites. Meanwhile, for recipes that state 'large eggs', these should weigh (still in their shells) about 63–73g (2½–2¾oz) and medium eggs should weigh 53g–63g (2–2½oz).

Chocolate: if chocolate is the dominant ingredient in a bake, it is definitely worth sourcing a good-quality brand – Callebaut, Valrhona and Pump Street are some of my favourites.

Yeast: the yeast used in these recipes is fast-action dried yeast. Unlike active dry yeast, it doesn't need to be bloomed in water and can be added to the dry ingredients straight away, unless otherwise stated in the recipe. It's worth remembering that it does have a shelf life and over time will lose its effectiveness.

Flour: it is important to use the type of flour stated in the recipe – plain, strong white or self-raising, unless alternatives are suggested. Be mindful that self-raising flour can age and thus lose its leavening capabilities. Strong flour has a higher protein (and therefore gluten) content; this makes it ideal for bread dough, which needs to expand and rise in order to produce a light aerated loaf or rolls. If possible, source quality flour from reputable mills; this will enhance the flavour profile of your bakes as well as supporting the environment.

Equipment

Using the right baking equipment really helps. Firstly, use the tin size instructed in the recipe – if you don't, the outcome will be altered, and usually not for the best. Secondly, fancy gadgets are not essential, but some things will make the baking experience a little easier. Here are my favourites.

A notebook: if you're a vaguely serious about baking, learn this lesson from me: make notes! Jot down exactly what you do as you bake so if things go a bit wrong, you can work back through what you did to establish where there might have been an error.

A simple set of digital scales: I know many people still work in cups, but I'm all about precision when it comes to baking. At the end of the day, it's a science, so the numbers matter.

Measuring spoons: these are great for accuracy with smaller measurements. A kitchen drawer staple in my opinion.

A simple balloon hand whisk: handy for making super-smooth sauces.

Spatulas: I'm a bit spatula-obsessed. I have many, but I'd recommend getting a big one and a small one as a minimum.

A microplane: this makes zesting and grating an absolute dream.

A selection of baking tins: loose-bottomed 15cm (6 inch) and 20cm (8 inch) round, square and fluted are the most traditional sizes used in recipes, so if you start with these, you should be able to take on a fair few bakes. A loaf tin is also super-handy – I find more recipes are written for 900g (2lb) loaf tins so I would opt for this first.

A selection of round pastry/cookie cutters: these can be handy, although they are not a total necessity. If you buy metal ones, make sure you dry them after washing them or they will go rusty.

Oven thermometer: oven temperatures vary, so grab yourself one of these. They're inexpensive and extremely useful to check that you're baking at the right temperature. For context, I know my oven is quite aggressive, which means I have to dial the temperature down a degree or two to ensure things

cook correctly. Incidentally, all the recipes in this book include both conventional and fan oven temperatures.

A digital thermometer: the simple ones aren't expensive, but I find them incredibly handy for double-checking whether things are baked. They're essential for certain caramels and chocolate/sugar work, too, if that becomes an interest for you.

A wire rack: to cool your bakes on.

Palette knifes: one large straight one and one smaller cranked one is all I have and all I need, but they are both excellent tools for all manner of things.

Reusable piping bags: not a necessity, but if you like to pipe things, then buying reusable piping bags is not only much better for the environment but they also don't tear as easily.

Beeswax wrap: I occasionally refer to cling film throughout the course of this book, and if you only have that, it obviously works; however, if you are keen to minimize plastic waste, then investing in some natural, reusable beeswax wraps is a great alternative.

A cake/icing smoother/scraper: essentially a piece of plastic to help you achieve a flawlessly smooth finish on your iced cakes.

Finally, and I know this is a big one, a stand mixer: I know how much of an investment this is (I remember when I got my first mini stand mixer years ago –I felt sick at the financial commitment at the time), but I promise you it will revolutionize your baking experience, and if you get a decent one, it will really last. Mine is still going strong – I can't recommend it enough.

Boost Your Confidence

If you have chosen to start at the beginning of this book,
you're more sensible than me! I typically engage with the pretty pictures, dive into a random recipe and before I know it, I've made a fundamental error – which is ultimately very annoying.

Baking is a multidimensional skill – it is dynamic and interactive and equips us with a wide range of competencies that can help to mitigate challenges posed in other areas of our lives. Not only is it creative, calming and meditative, it is educational, coaches us in the art of patience and produces a product that makes us feel fulfilled. If we are feeling defeated, a little baking triumph can be a reminder to ourselves that we can produce something good, and it can make us feel more confident to tackle other challenges in life.

The recipes in this chapter are here to provide you with a good grounding. They're not all super-simple – I still sweat every time I make choux pastry (see page 28), my cake batter sometimes splits when I add the eggs (see page 41) and any yeasted product has the potential to develop a mind of its own given a half chance (see page 32) – but they are all achievable with a little resolve.

Whether you are a seasoned baker or complete novice, sometimes a boost of self-confidence is necessary. Even after a few years of baking, I frequently experience moments of insecurity or worry related to a particular aspect of baking. In these instances, I have to walk away for a day or so, gather myself together and then cautiously 'get back on the horse'! I always return to the kitchen with a fresh head, a plan, a simple recipe – either in time taken, execution or number or ingredients – and less pressure on myself.

Similarly, if you are new to baking, starting with some of the basics can be helpful to both build confidence and help you get to grips with some of the processes involved in baking. It's a chance to establish how your oven operates – does it run a bit cold or hot? – and determine what cake batter looks like when it's been mixed perfectly versus when the eggs have curdled. The outcome will taste good regardless, but you can be as inquisitive as you desire. Consider the time spent on these bakes as a learning experience, shift your mindset from perfection to pretty good and make notes on how you can improve things next time. It's time to be a sponge: soak up all the information your kitchen throws at you.

Ultimately, self-confidence is the basis for success. If confidence is your strength already, then these bakes may represent quick wins for you, but if you need a little boost, a cookie or a tasty chocolate biscuit may be all you need to prime you for a lifetime of joyful baking success.

Comté and Nutmeg Puffs

Makes
14 puffs

Hands-on time
30 minutes

Cooking time
20–25 minutes

It may become obvious that I really love cheese. The stronger the better, always room temperature or warmer, ideally melted... add a carbohydrate and you have yourself a meal, to be eaten at any time of day and in any climate.

This recipe really captures my cheesy love affair in one mouthful – bite-size, puffy, cheese-scented clouds. They are simple in concept yet punchy in flavour, comprised of a simple choux pastry dough topped with Comté cheese and optional seeds. They are a real crowd-pleasing canapé for a dinner party or, if you're like me, a fabulous snack to rustle up when you're in need of a little baking Zen.

60ml (2½fl oz) whole milk

60ml (2½fl oz) water

55g (2¼oz) unsalted butter

½ tsp sea salt

½ tsp caster sugar

60g (2½oz) plain flour, sifted

2 large eggs, lightly beaten

¼–½ tsp freshly grated nutmeg (optional)

Topping

50g (2oz) Comté, grated

Poppy seeds, nigella seeds or sesame seeds, for sprinkling (optional)

Preheat the oven to 200°C/180°C fan/400°F/Gas 6. Line a large baking tray with baking parchment.

Combine the milk, water, butter, salt and sugar in a medium saucepan. Place over a low heat and allow the butter to melt while stirring occasionally. Once melted, increase the heat and bring to the boil.

Once boiling, temporarily remove from the heat and tip in the sifted flour, then beat with a wooden spoon until a smooth dough forms. Place back over a medium-low heat and continue to stir until the mixture starts to dry out and pull away from the sides of the pan – about 2 minutes.

Scrape the dough into a large heatproof bowl and allow to cool for 1 minute, then add the eggs to the dough little by little, beating thoroughly between each addition. It will initially look curdled after you add the egg, but persevere with the beating and it will come together. Once all the egg has been incorporated, add the grated nutmeg and stir it through the dough.

Transfer the dough to a piping bag fitted with a large round nozzle and pipe small blobs onto the lined baking tray, spaced about 2cm (¾in)

apart (alternatively, use two very lightly oiled teaspoons to scoop evenly sized blobs onto the baking tray). Use a damp finger to smooth off any peaks of dough. Sprinkle with the cheese and seeds, if using.

Bake in the oven for 22–25 minutes, or until puffed up and golden brown.

Once baked, remove from the oven and pierce the bottom of each cheese puff with the tip of a large knife or a skewer to allow the steam to escape.

Transfer to a wire rack. Ideally these are eaten warm, but if any are left over, allow them to cool completely before storing.

Notes

These are best eaten straight away but can be kept in an airtight container for several days – just crisp them up in the oven for about 5 minutes at 180°C/160°C fan/350°F/Gas 4 before eating.

I'd always suggest a strong cheese here, but use your imagination in terms of what you go for – a blue cheese and crushed walnut affair would work a treat!

You could also try adding alternative spices through the pastry dough. Try garam masala, ground cumin and/or coriander topped with nigella seeds for an Indian twist. Paprika or cayenne pepper and Cheddar are a wonderful marriage, too. Or go for za'atar and sesame seeds for a Middle Eastern vibe.

Comfort Bread

This bread is the epitome of comfort baking – a literal hug in a loaf. Assign yourself a morning of baking therapy and get lost in a mindful session of kneading, proving, shaping and baking. It's the perfect antidote to our frenetic society's tendency to rush, stress and fuss over things. Not only does this bread taste sensational – with or without its secret ingredient, Marmite – it stimulates all the other senses, too, with its pillowy soft dough, Twiglet-like aroma while baking and tender, delicate crust that shatters when sliced. This masterpiece is best served with butter and more Marmite, a mountain of cheese and pickle, or topped with a heap of mature Cheddar then melted under the grill and smeared with English mustard (toasties are also an excellent option).

Makes
1 loaf

Hands-on time
20 minutes + 2 hours
proving time

Cooking time
45 minutes

Combine the cream and milk in a bowl or large jug and add the lemon juice. Stir, then set aside for 5 minutes.

Meanwhile, put the flour into a large bowl and add the salt to one side of the bowl and the yeast to the other.

Next, add the cold water and the just-boiled water to the cream mixture, then add the butter, Marmite and honey and use a whisk or spatula to combine. Allow to cool to 35°C (95°F) – it should feel lukewarm.

Once cooled, add the liquids to the dry ingredients. Use a spatula or wooden spoon to bring the ingredients together into a shaggy dough. Once combined, cover with a damp tea towel and leave to rest for 20 minutes at room temperature (this is the autolyse stage).

Once rested, lightly smear your hands and the work surface with a little oil and remove the dough from the bowl, then knead the dough for 5 minutes. Return the dough to the bowl, cover, and rest for a further 10 minutes. After this second rest, remove the dough from the bowl once more. It should feel notably smoother. Knead for 5 minutes until it is glossy and elastic.

45ml (1¾fl oz) single cream, cold

55ml (2¼fl oz) whole milk

1 tsp lemon juice

500g (1lb 2oz) strong white bread flour, plus extra for dusting

5g (1 tsp) sea salt (increase to 10g/2 tsp if omitting the Marmite)

7g (¼oz) sachet of fast-action dried yeast

140ml (4¾fl oz) cold water

100ml (3½fl oz) just-boiled water

20g (¾oz) unsalted butter, softened

25g (1oz) Marmite

15g (½oz) honey

Vegetable oil, for greasing

Transfer the dough to a well oiled bowl, cover and leave to prove for 1 hour in a warm (and humid, if possible) environment until approximately doubled in size.

Grease a deep-sided 900g (2lb) loaf tin and line with baking parchment. Once risen, punch down the dough, then turn out onto a lightly floured work surface and pat into an approximate rectangle around 2.5cm (1in) thick.

Starting on one of the longer sides, roll the dough up tightly like a scroll. Pinch the dough together at the seam and place in the tin, seam side down. Cover and leave to rise for 45 minutes to 1 hour until it has increased in size by about three-quarters.

Around 30 minutes before you intend to bake your loaf, preheat the oven to 200°C/180°C fan/400°F/Gas 6. Place a shallow tray in the bottom of the oven.

Once sufficiently proved, transfer the loaf to the oven and pour a cup of boiling water into the tray at the bottom. Bake for 30 minutes, then carefully remove the loaf from the oven, gently tap off the tin and peel away the baking parchment.

Return the loaf to the oven and continue to bake for a further 15 minutes, or until golden and hollow sounding when tapped underneath. Leave to cool on a wire rack.

Notes

To create a humid environment for your dough to prove, place it in a cold oven with a tray or bowl containing an inch or so of boiling water. Close the door to create a mini sauna.

This loaf has a dark crust due to the Marmite, so don't worry if it looks a bit 'overdone' towards the end of the baking time.

To double-check that your loaf is baked, use a digital thermometer. It should read 95°C/203°F when inserted into the centre of the loaf.

Marmite haters, don't panic! Firstly, it's a subtle flavour, imparting just a savoury note, however, if you really can't bear it, omit it entirely and increase the quantity of salt – you will still be rewarded with the most perfect slice of doorstep toast.

Middle Eastern-style Quick Flatbreads with Two Dips

Alfresco summer lunches are incomplete without warm, slightly blistered flatbreads; either stuffed with fillings (falafel for me), heaped with hummus, tzatziki or guacamole, or simply sprinkled with sea salt and doused in olive oil. I usually prefer yeasted breads, but these quick, unleavened flatbreads are perfect for when you don't have time to wait for yeast to do its thing. They are layered with olive oil and spices for a wonderful flavour and flaky texture.

Serves
4

Hands-on time
15 minutes + 20 minutes resting time

Cooking time
8–10 minutes per flatbread

~~~~~~~~~~~~~~~~~~~~~~~~~~~~~

220g (7¾oz) plain flour, plus extra for dusting

30g (1¼oz) gram (chickpea) flour

¾ tsp sea salt

1 tsp caster sugar

10ml (2 tsp) extra virgin olive oil

130ml (4½fl oz) just-boiled water

Vegetable oil, for greasing and frying

Filling

20g (¾oz) plain flour

60ml (2½fl oz) extra virgin olive oil

Pinch of ground black pepper

Pinch of ground cardamom

Pinch of cayenne pepper

2 tsp ground cumin

1 tsp ground coriander

2 garlic cloves, grated

2 tbsp finely chopped parsley

Pinch of salt

Squeeze of lemon juice

Lemon and garlic tahini dipping sauce

1 tbsp lemon juice

1 small garlic clove, crushed or grated

30g (1¼oz) tahini

⅛ tsp sea salt

Pinch of ground cumin

Pinch of black pepper

About 1½ tbsp ice-cold water

Cucumber and herb raita

125g (4¼oz) full-fat Greek yoghurt

25ml (1fl oz) whole milk

½ small shallot, finely chopped

Squeeze of lime juice

25g (1oz) cucumber, deseeded and very finely diced

⅛ tsp fine sea salt

¼ tsp runny honey

½ tbsp finely chopped coriander

½ tbsp finely chopped mint leaves

¼ tsp cumin seeds

Combine the plain flour, gram flour, salt and sugar in a large bowl and lightly whisk together. Drizzle over the oil, followed by the water. Use your hands or a spatula to bring the ingredients together into a shaggy dough. It may seem quite sticky at first. Transfer to a work surface and knead for 5 minutes until smooth, pliable and no longer sticky. Transfer back to the bowl, cover and leave to rest for 20 minutes while you prepare the filling.

In a small bowl, combine the flour and oil, and stir until homogenous. Add the remaining ingredients and stir to combine, then set aside until ready to use.

Next prepare the dipping sauces. For the lemon and garlic tahini dipping sauce, combine the lemon juice and garlic in a small bowl and leave to infuse for 10 minutes. Once infused, add the tahini, salt, cumin and black pepper and stir until well combined. Finally, whisk in the ice-cold water 1 teaspoon at a time until you have a smooth sauce – don't worry if the mixture splits or thickens, continue to slowly add the water and you will achieve a perfect creamy consistency. Cover and set aside until ready to use.

For the cucumber and herb raita, combine the yoghurt, milk, shallot, lime juice, cucumber, salt, honey, coriander and mint in a small bowl. Leave to stand in the fridge for a minimum of 20 minutes, or this can be left overnight for even more flavour.

Once the flatbread dough has rested, transfer it to a very lightly oiled work surface and divide into four balls of about 95g (3¼oz). Take one dough ball (leave the remainder covered with a damp tea towel until ready to use) and roll out as thin as you can without tearing – around a 30cm (12in) diameter is perfect. Spread a quarter of the filling (about 25g/1oz) over the surface of the dough using a pastry brush. Starting at one side, tightly roll up the dough to form a thin log, then coil up the log to form a spiral shape. Press the end into the side of the spiral to seal it off.

Once the dough is coiled, lightly dust the work surface with a little flour. Press down on top of the spiral before using a rolling pin to roll it out into a circle, approximately 20cm (8in) in diameter. Continually rotate the dough as you roll it to achieve a neat, round shape. Cover loosely with a tea towel. Repeat with the remaining dough balls.

Drizzle a little oil into a non-stick frying pan and set over a medium heat. Once hot, add the flatbreads to the pan one at a time and cook for 3–4 minutes on each side, or until golden brown. Once cooked, transfer the flatbreads to a wire rack lined with a little kitchen paper and cover with a tea towel to stop it drying out. Repeat with the remaining dough balls.

When ready to serve, warm a dry frying pan over a medium heat and lightly toast the cumin seeds for the raita. When they start to pop, remove from the pan, crush in a pestle and mortar and sprinkle over the raita.

Note

There are countless other flavour ideas you can try with this recipe, but these are my favourites:

Korean style – switch the gram flour for fine semolina and try sesame oil instead of olive oil for the filling, combined with a little Sichuan pepper and a handful of spring onions. Serve with a sweet chilli sauce.

Za'atar filled – again, switch the gram flour for fine semolina and use about 2 tablespoons za'atar in the filling. Serve with hummus.

Mum's Sticky Gingerbread with Brandy Toffee Apples

Serves
9

Hands-on time
20 minutes

Cooking time
50–60 minutes

It's no secret that my mum has never been drawn to the kitchen – in fact, she quite likes it kept clean, neat and tidy. Nevertheless, she's got a talent for just about anything and baking is no exception. She must have mentioned this gingerbread recipe to me on countless occasions, but every time I brushed it off as being 'old fashioned' and boring... well, I was wrong... it's wildly wicked. Spiked with a hint of warming gingery spice, light as candy floss and moist for days, this super-simple to prepare cake is a winner. What makes this cake even better is its adaptability; it's perfect as is for afternoon tea, or can be served as a dinner-party pudding, paired with brandy toffee apples and a hefty dollop of crème fraîche.

50g (2oz) black treacle
50g (2oz) golden syrup
120g (4oz) light brown muscovado sugar
120g (4oz) unsalted butter
175g (6oz) plain flour
¼ tsp sea salt
1 tbsp ground ginger
1½ tsp ground cinnamon
1 large egg, lightly beaten
140ml (4¾fl oz) whole milk
1 tsp bicarbonate of soda
120g (4oz) crème fraîche, to serve (optional)

Brandy Toffee Apples

2 medium Pink Lady apples (about 200g/7oz), peeled, cored and cut into 1cm (½in) slices
35ml (1¼fl oz) double cream
1 tbsp brandy
½ tbsp lemon juice
25g (1oz) unsalted butter
25g (1oz) dark brown muscovado sugar
1 tsp black treacle

Notes

Mum also mentioned that when she used to bake this at university, she and her friends would cool the cake in a cake storage tin – apparently it yields the stickiest masterpiece. Just leave it in the baking tin when it comes out of the oven and immediately transfer it to a heatproof airtight container.

This is the perfect autumn/ winter bake. From September to December, I love using apples picked from my neighbour's tree – they are so perfectly sweet yet crisp. If you can find some in-season British apples they're always going to top any other variety; just make sure they're sweet eating apples, not cooking apples.

Preheat the oven to 150°C/130°C fan/300°F/Gas 2. Grease an 18cm (7in) square tin and line with baking parchment.

Put the treacle, golden syrup, sugar and butter into a large saucepan and melt over a gentle heat. Sift the flour, salt, ginger and cinnamon into a bowl and gently mix to combine. Fold the dry ingredients into the wet ingredients in three stages. Beat in the egg.

Warm the milk a little, add the bicarbonate of soda and lightly whisk to combine, then gently stir the milk mixture into the batter until homogenous and you have a syrupy, loose batter – be patient, it takes a bit of persistence.

Pour into the prepared tin and bake in the oven for 50–60 minutes. Once cooked, remove from the oven and leave to cool completely in the tin.

Next make the toffee apples. Place a non-stick frying pan over a medium heat, add the apples and sear each side for about 2 minutes. Remove from the heat.

Pour the cream, brandy and lemon juice into a small jug. Combine the butter, sugar and treacle in a small saucepan over a low heat, stirring to combine; once a syrupy mixture has formed, stir in the cream mixture. Bring to a bubbling boil over a medium heat and simmer for 2–3 minutes, stirring constantly. Remove from the heat and set aside to cool a little.

Finally, add the apples and leave to infuse for at least 30 minutes, if possible. Gently reheat the apples before serving with the cake and crème fraîche, if using.

Spiced Spelt, Fruit and Oat Cookies

Most people's first thought when it comes to cookies is usually chocolate chip, and let's face it, they have earned their crown in the cookie world. However, I think oatmeal and raisin is a forgotten wonder and deserves greater respect. There's something incredibly comforting about them – the fruit, added texture of oats and subtle hint of spice adds another dimension to the whole concept of a cookie.

In name, these cookies sound like another one of those 'healthy' or 'superfood' concepts, but don't be fooled, they're a somewhat pimped-up version of the humble classic we know and love. They just happen to be packed with some pretty wholesome ingredients that add texture, depth and flavour.

Makes
14 cookies

Hands-on time
20 minutes + 2 hours chilling

Cooking time
17–20 minutes per batch

70g (2¾oz) soft light brown sugar

70g (2¾oz) golden caster sugar

115g (3¾oz) unsalted butter, softened

Zest of ½ orange

40g (1½oz) honey

½ tsp freshly grated nutmeg

½–¾ tsp ground cinnamon

¼ tsp baking powder

½ tsp bicarbonate of soda

½ tsp sea salt

1 large egg

½ tsp vanilla extract

85g (3oz) spelt flour, sifted

40g (1½oz) wholemeal flour, sifted

100g (3½oz) jumbo rolled oats

50g (2oz) rolled oats (not quick oats)

70g (2¾oz) sultanas

30g (1¼oz) dried cranberries

20g (¾oz) pumpkin seeds

20g (¾oz) mixed seeds (linseed/sesame seeds/ sunflower seeds)

Note

If you rest the cookie dough for longer than 2 hours, it can be a little tough to remove from the bowl – allow it to come to room temperature for around 15 minutes before using an ice cream scoop or spoon to dig out cookie dough portions.

Combine the sugars, butter, orange zest, honey, nutmeg, cinnamon, baking powder, bicarbonate of soda and salt in a large bowl and beat with an electric hand mixer for about 3 minutes until light and fluffy. Scrape down the sides and bottom before adding the egg and vanilla, then beat again.

Gently mix in the flours on the lowest speed (or by hand), and once almost combined, add the oats, then the fruit and seeds. Mix until just combined. Check everything has been incorporated, then cover and chill for 2 hours.

Preheat the oven to 180°C/160°C fan/350°F/Gas 4 and place two baking trays inside to preheat.

Remove the chilled dough from the fridge. Scoop out 50g (2oz) chunks of dough and shape into loose balls.

Remove the baking trays from the oven and line with baking parchment. Transfer the cookie dough balls to the lined sheets, placed about 5cm (2in) apart.

Bake for 17–20 minutes until deep golden at the edges and slightly paler in the middle. After about 12 minutes of baking, remove the baking trays from the oven and give them a firm tap on the work surface to slightly collapse the cookies. Repeat this process at 15 minutes.

Once baked, remove the cookies from the oven, give the sheets a final tap on the work surface and leave to firm up for 5 minutes before transferring to a wire rack to cool. Repeat with the remaining cookies, remembering to preheat a third baking tray before baking the final batch if necessary.

The Queen of Cakes

I know you'll all have your own Victoria sponge recipes, passed down from Mum/Grandad/Auntie Mavis, and you're thinking, *Steph, really? We don't need another version of this simple classic.* Except, I didn't have a recipe that was passed down to me – my baking epiphany came later in life, and so I've had to conjure up my own. So, for anyone else who's new to baking and lacking a family hand-me-down, I'm here to save the day.

While the classic Victoria sponge has somewhat lost its crown of late, eclipsed by its more decadent counterparts, I still find its simplicity and legacy almost unrivalled. My version consists of a light, buttery, vanilla sponge, drizzled with a little lime and mint syrup, layered with a roasted strawberry jam that tastes so strawberry-y, you won't quite believe it, and finished with pillowy soft Chantilly cream; it's worth a try even if your grandma's is unbeatable.

This is a blank canvas for you to explore the world of Victoria sponges – switch up your jam, alter the sponge flavouring with a little almond or lemon; the world really is your oyster.

Serves
10–12

Hands-on time
30 minutes

Cooking time
30–35 minutes, 1½ hours + macerating time for the jam

250g (9oz) unsalted butter, softened

250g (9oz) caster sugar

1 tsp vanilla extract

250g (9oz) self-raising flour

¼ tsp salt

¼ tsp bicarbonate of soda

4 large eggs

50ml (2fl oz) whole milk

Roasted strawberry 'jam'

400g (14oz) fresh strawberries, hulled and quartered

50g (2oz) caster sugar

15ml (1 tbsp) lime juice

Syrup

40ml (1½fl oz) lime juice

40g (1½oz) caster sugar

5 mint leaves

Chantilly cream

300ml (10½fl oz) double cream

15g (½oz) icing sugar

½ tsp vanilla bean paste

Decoration

100g (3½oz) fresh strawberries

Handful of mint leaves

First make the roasted strawberry jam. Place the strawberries in a bowl and add the caster sugar and lime juice. Leave the fruit to macerate for 30 minutes, or overnight. When ready to cook, preheat the oven to 150°C/130°C fan/300°F/Gas 2 and line a baking tray with baking parchment.

Spread the strawberries out onto the lined baking tray and roast in the oven for 1½ hours, stirring every 30 minutes. Once the strawberries have darkened and are syrupy, remove from the oven. If you like, you can mash up any big lumps of strawberry with a fork. Leave to cool before covering and transferring to the fridge.

Meanwhile, prepare the sponge. Preheat the oven to 180°C/160°C fan/350°F/Gas 4. Grease and line two 20cm (8in) round cake tins (or four 15cm/6in tins).

Combine the butter, sugar and vanilla extract in a large bowl and beat until very pale, fluffy and increased in volume, scraping down the sides of the bowl as necessary. Meanwhile, sift the flour into a large bowl, add the salt and bicarbonate of soda and mix to combine.

Gradually beat the eggs into the butter mixture, making sure each one is fully incorporated before adding the next. Once homogenous, fold in the dry ingredients in two stages, before folding in the milk, again in two stages.

Once everything is fully combined, distribute the batter evenly between the two cake tins and level with a palette knife. Bake in the oven for 25–30 minutes (or 20–25 minutes if using smaller tins).

While the cakes bake, prepare the sugar syrup. Combine the sugar and lime juice in a saucepan. Place over a low heat and stir until the sugar dissolves. Once the sugar has dissolved, increase the heat, bring to the boil and simmer for 1 minute.

Notes

I've used the creaming method above. It unquestionably produces the lightest sponge, with a tender crumb and beautiful rise; however, it's critical that you take your time with this method. Here are a few technique tips:

Firstly, ensure your ingredients are all room temperature – that's around 20°C (68°F).

A stand mixer really helps you out here, but an electric hand mixer is more than adequate.

When recipes tell you to beat the butter and sugar until light and fluffy, they mean it – it should be very pale, fluffy and increased in volume. A good 5–10 minutes isn't unreasonable. Beat on a medium-high speed; too high and you create large air pockets that weaken the structure of your sponge.

Add the eggs slowly to prevent them from curdling; ensure each addition is fully incorporated with the butter mixture before continuing.

If your mixture does look curdled, it's not the end of the world – a spoonful of the flour mixture beaten in can help bring it back a bit, then continue to add the remaining flour as directed.

Remove from the heat, add the mint leaves – making sure they are fully submerged – and set aside to cool.

Once baked, remove the cakes from the oven and leave to cool in the tins for 5 minutes before turning out onto a wire rack to cool fully.

Meanwhile, combine the ingredients for the Chantilly cream in a bowl and beat to medium-stiff peaks. Do this on a super-low speed – it takes a bit longer, but it gives you a more stable whipped cream and reduces the risk of over-whipping.

To assemble, place the first sponge layer on a cake board or serving board and brush over a thin layer of sugar syrup. Spread with roasted strawberry jam before dolloping or piping on the Chantilly cream. Add the next layer of sponge, flat side up, and add another layer of cream, then garnish with the fresh strawberries and mint leaves. If you're not so fussed about tons of fresh cream, omit from the top and simply dust with caster sugar.

Variations

The main recipe uses the low and slow approach to this queen of cakes, but there are other less arduous ways of producing a similarly delectable result. Go for the all-in-one method: add the butter, sugar, eggs, flour, bicarbonate of soda and salt to a mixer or bowl. Beat on a medium-high speed for around a minute until well incorporated, scrape around the bowl, then mix again on a lower speed as you add the milk and vanilla extract and continue to beat for 20 seconds until fully combined. The sponges may dome a little more when baked but will still be ever so light and moist!

If you're tight for time, there's an alternative jam option, too. Increase the sugar to 100g (3½oz). Macerate the fruit as before, for 30 minutes, to help dissolve the sugar and improve the flavour, then pour the mixture into a medium-sized pan and place over a medium heat. Bring to a simmer before reducing the heat. Continue to cook, stirring periodically, until the mixture has thickened considerably – around 10–15 minutes. For a smooth texture, sieve out the little seeds. Set aside to cool.

If you choose to do a towering four-layer 15cm (6in) cake, bear in mind that the height does compromise its stability a bit, so take care on assembly. Alternatively, you could make three-quarters of the recipe and make a three-layer cake, which will be equally impressive but a little more stable.

Boozy Baked Peaches with Crunchy Amaretti Biscuits

Serves
4

Hands-on time
20 minutes + drying and overnight thickening time

Cooking time
60 minutes

I'm frequently asked what my favourite bake is. Sometimes, people get specific and narrow it down to a genre of baking – then I know they mean business and that I need to really consider my answer! Generally, I think this is the kind of question for which my answer varies with the seasons, my mood and the environment. Warm weather involves something fruity and cooling, cold and dark days call for warming scents and piping hot, steaming decadence. However, there is one type of dessert that I would opt for over almost anything else in any climate and under any circumstance, and that is warm fruit paired with a rich and almost tangy cream product and some nutty or biscuity crunch. I have fond memories of such desserts being served up after dinner with my grandparents, and still nothing beats it.

So, here I present you with an adult version of this simple to prepare, crowd-pleasing miracle combination. Steaming, soft, juicy peaches, elevated with amaretto liqueur and spices, served with crème fraîche (homemade if you can be bothered) and topped with crunchy crushed amaretti biscuits. Honestly, comfort in a bowl.

90ml (3¼fl oz) amaretto

30ml (1¼fl oz) orange juice

30g (1¼oz) golden caster sugar

1 tsp vanilla extract

4 ripe peaches, halved and stoned

5 cardamom pods

Homemade crème fraîche

115ml (3¾fl oz) pasteurized double cream

20ml (¾fl oz) buttermilk

Amaretti (makes 6 biscuits)

45g (1¾oz) ground almonds

50g (2oz) caster sugar

1 large egg white

½ tsp almond extract

Flaked almonds, for the tops

The day before, prepare the crème fraîche. Combine the cream and buttermilk in a bowl and leave at room temperature or somewhere warm in your house – ideally 22–25°C (72–77°F) – for 12–24 hours. Once thickened, refrigerate until ready to use.

Next, prepare the amaretti. Preheat the oven to 170°C/150°C fan/325°F/Gas 3 and line a baking tray with baking parchment.

Combine the almonds and caster sugar in a bowl, add the almond extract and set aside. In a separate bowl, using an electric hand mixer, beat the egg white to stiff peaks. Fold the egg white through the almond mixture in two stages. Scoop out 20g (¾oz) spoonfuls of the mixture and dollop onto the baking tray, spaced well apart. Top each biscuit with a pinch of flaked almonds.

Note

Apricots would be an excellent alternative fruit here, but bear in mind they cook a bit quicker so adjust the cooking time accordingly.

Bake for 40 minutes, or until golden brown. Turn the oven off, open the door slightly (I wedge mine with a wooden spoon to stop it from closing) and leave the amaretti to cool inside the oven for 2 hours, or overnight. Once cooled, store in an airtight container.

Half an hour before you plan to serve, preheat the oven to 200°C/180°C fan/400°F/Gas 6.

Combine the amaretto, orange juice, sugar and vanilla. Place the peaches cut side up in a ceramic baking dish. Pour over the amaretto mixture, sprinkle with the cardamom pods and bake for 20 minutes, or until tender but holding their shape – this will depend on the ripeness of your peaches; if they start to brown, cover with foil and continue to bake until tender, but keep any eye on them as they can go from underdone to mush in minutes.

Once the peaches have baked, remove them from the oven and allow to cool slightly before carefully peeling off their skins. Transfer to a plate along with plenty of the juices. Add a hefty dollop of the crème fraîche and crumble over the amaretti biscuits. Dive in!

Boozy Vegan Truffles Two Ways

There have been certain times in my life when I have felt utter despair, often triggered by seemingly inconsequential circumstances. In these moments, baking that involves any degree of attention to detail, concentration or labour just isn't really appropriate. However, in these dark moments, I still seem to seek out the comfort of the kitchen and one of my go-to recipes is truffles. There's something especially mindful, soothing and gratifying about preparing these simple nuggets of joy. Below are my two favourite takes on a chocolate truffle – both happen to be vegan, although any good-quality chocolate will more than suffice. The first version happens to pack a decent fibre punch, but most importantly they both do wonders for the soul, both in preparation and consumption – consider them 'bake yourself better' truffles.

Makes
10 truffles

Hands-on time
20 minutes + 1 hour setting time

Date, Almond and Rum Truffles

Combine the dates, maple syrup and rum in a high-speed blender and blend until smooth, then add the coconut oil and blend to combine. Next add the cocoa powder and continue to blend to a paste. Finally add the ground almonds and pulse to combine – don't blend too much or the almonds will start to release some of their oils and the truffles will be oily.

Once everything is combined, tip the mixture into a bowl, then divide into roughly 15g (½oz) chunks and roll into balls.

To make the chocolate coating, put the chocolate into a small heatproof bowl and set it over a pan of gently simmering water to melt. Once melted, whisk in the coconut oil to form a smooth and glossy chocolate coating. Dunk the truffle balls in the coating, using a spoon to spin them round in the chocolate before transferring to a plate. If you like, you can sprinkle the truffles with a little desiccated coconut at this point, before the chocolate sets.

Once all the balls are coated in chocolate, transfer to the fridge to set before serving. These will keep in an airtight container in the fridge for about a week or in the freezer for a month.

75g (2¾oz) pitted Medjool dates

½ tbsp maple syrup

1 tbsp dark rum (or liquor of your choice/orange juice)

½ tbsp coconut oil

15g (½oz) cocoa powder

50g (2oz) ground almonds

Chocolate coating

75g (2¾oz) good-quality vegan dark chocolate

1 tsp coconut oil

Desiccated coconut, for sprinkling (optional)

Coconut and Rum Truffles

100g (3½oz) good-quality
    vegan dark chocolate
1 tsp coconut oil
80g (3oz) coconut cream
1 tbsp dark rum
10g (¼oz) cocoa powder

Makes
12 truffles

Hands-on time
10 minutes + overnight
setting

Combine the chocolate and coconut oil in a medium-sized heatproof bowl and set to one side. Combine the coconut cream and rum in a small saucepan, place over a medium heat and bring almost to the boil. Remove from the heat and pour over the chocolate and oil mixture, making sure all of the chocolate is covered.

Let it stand for a couple of minutes before gently stirring until the ingredients are fully combined and a smooth glossy ganache forms. Allow to cool before transferring to the fridge to set for at least 12 hours. Once set, remove from the fridge.

Shake the cocoa powder onto a small plate. Divide the ganache into roughly 15g (½oz) chunks and roll into balls. Roll each ball in cocoa powder and transfer to a plate. Once all the balls are coated in chocolate, transfer to the fridge to set before serving. These will keep in an airtight container in the fridge for about a week or in the freezer for a month.

Notes

A pair of food handling gloves can be useful to prevent you from getting the ganache everywhere.

Try a different booze for an alternative flavour.

Prune and Armagnac Fondant Brownies

Makes
16 small squares

Hands-on time
20 minutes + 1 hour soaking time

Cooking time
40 minutes

A recipe book dedicated to baking and happiness must involve a brownie, right? To be truthful, I wouldn't say I'm a 'chocoholic' at all – in fact, as a kid, I could take or leave the stuff. But brownies have an amazing ability to offer a little comfort in pretty much any scenario. Stressed? Upset? Anxious? Cold? The brownie has your back. Even when we're happy, in love or celebrating, it can add a little something extra.

I love my bulletproof brownie recipe from *The Joy of Baking*, but this is a little something extra. Eaten when still warm, it's oozy and gooey like a fondant. Rich prunes soaked in brandy (Armagnac in this instance) are the perfect accompaniment to dark chocolate and they really enhance the flavour of these brownies – no longer just a chocolatey snack, they become a slightly devilish mouthful of soul-soothing joy. Finally, I use ground almonds instead of flour for even more flavour and texture.

125g (4¼oz) pitted prunes, chopped

20ml (4 tsp) Armagnac

165g (5¾oz) unsalted butter

235g (8¼oz) good-quality dark chocolate

3 large eggs

100g (3½oz) caster sugar

135g (4½oz) soft light brown sugar

75g (2¾oz) ground almonds

35g (1¼oz) good-quality cocoa powder

¼–½ tsp fine sea salt

Ice cream or cream, to serve (optional)

Combine the prunes and Armagnac in a bowl and leave to soak for at least 1 hour.

Preheat the oven to 180°C/160°C fan/350°F/Gas 4 and grease and line a 20cm (8in) square tin with baking parchment.

Put the butter and chocolate into a heatproof bowl and place over a pan filled with about 2.5cm (1in) simmering water. Allow to melt, stirring occasionally. Once melted, set aside to cool for 5–10 minutes.

Meanwhile, combine the eggs and sugars in a large bowl. Beat with an electric hand mixer for 5–6 minutes until pale, frothy and increased in volume.

Next, sift the ground almonds, cocoa powder and salt into a bowl and set aside.

Note

Once the chocolate and butter have cooled a little, add to the egg mixture in two stages, gently folding through to combine. Next, carefully fold through the dry ingredients before finally folding in the boozy prunes, trying not to overmix at either stage. Pour into the prepared tin and bake for around 40 minutes, or until it is slightly risen, with a thin, shiny crust that is fairly firm, but soft and gooey in the centre.

Once baked, remove the brownie from the oven and allow to cool for a minimum of 30 minutes. Enjoy while still warm with ice cream or cream or leave to cool completely – the longer they are left to 'set', the more fudgy they will become.

The Ultimate Chocolate Biscuit

Is there a more quintessentially British delicacy than a biscuit and a cuppa? The ritual of putting the kettle on for a cup of tea or coffee, reaching into the biscuit jar for your favourite biscuit to dunk (or not?) and savouring those 15 minutes of your day is unrivalled; it's comfort, a break from work, nostalgia, a snack and a pick-me-up for mind and body. Of course, our supermarket favourites are great, but creating your very own version provides an extra level of joy; whether you call it emotional support, therapy, mindfulness or just a bit of creativity and fun, it delivers. Not only that, when you're using quality ingredients to make your own biscuits, you can be confident that you're creating a more nutritious alternative to the shop-bought varieties.

My version is somewhere between oat biscuit and digestive; it's short yet crisp and the malt extract and rye flour give the biscuits a distinct earthiness and nuttiness. Sandwiched between two thin biscuits is a layer of smooth truffle-y ganache, providing a textural contrast and complementary level of sophisticated indulgence.

Makes
10–12 biscuits

Hands-on time
40 minutes + 1¼ hours chilling time

Cooking time
10–12 minutes

100g (3½oz) rolled oats
35g (1¼oz) rye flour
30g (1oz) plain flour
40g (1½oz) light brown muscovado sugar
¼ tsp bicarbonate of soda
¼ tsp sea salt
55g (2¼oz) cold unsalted butter, cubed
½ tsp white wine vinegar
½ tsp malt extract
55g (2¼oz) unsalted butter, melted

Ganache
100g (3½oz) milk chocolate
50ml (2fl oz) double cream

Combine the oats, flours, sugar, bicarbonate of soda and salt in a food processor and pulse until you have a fine mealy consistency, then transfer to a large bowl. Add the cubed butter and rub into the dry ingredients until the mixture resembles breadcrumbs.

Add the vinegar and malt extract to the melted butter and stir well to combine before pouring into the crumb mixture. Stir with a spatula – the mixture should start to come together – then get your hands into the bowl and bring it together to form a dough.

Tip out onto a large rectangle of baking parchment and place another piece of parchment the same size on top. Roll out to a thickness of around 3mm (⅛in). Place the sheet of dough on a baking tray and refrigerate for 20 minutes.

Meanwhile, line two baking trays with baking parchment. Once the dough is chilled, remove it from the fridge and peel away the top layer of parchment. Use a 6cm (2¼in) cookie cutter (fluted or round) to stamp out an even number of rounds, re-rolling the dough between the parchment until it is all used up. I can usually yield around 20–24.

Arrange the rounds on the lined baking trays and use a round 2cm (¾in) cutter to stamp out the centre of half of the rounds – these will be the top of your sandwich biscuits (you can bake the little centre pieces of dough with the rest of the biscuits; they are a wonderful snack while you're baking). Refrigerate the biscuits for at least 1 hour.

Preheat the oven to 190°C/170°C fan/375°F/Gas 5. Once rested, bake the biscuits for 10–11 minutes, or until golden. Remove from the oven and leave to cool for 5 minutes on the tray before transferring to a wire rack to cool completely.

Meanwhile, prepare the ganache. Put the chocolate in a heatproof bowl. In a small saucepan, warm the double cream until almost boiling, then pour over the chocolate. Allow to sit for 1 minute before stirring to combine. If there is still some unmelted chocolate, set the bowl over a pan of barely simmering water and heat very gently, stirring constantly, until a smooth, glossy ganache forms. Allow to cool for 10–15 minutes.

Once the biscuits and ganache have cooled, dollop a teaspoon of ganache in the centre of the whole round biscuits and spread out a little using the back of the spoon, not taking it too near the edges. Press one of the topping biscuits on top. Repeat with the remaining biscuits.

Note

If you are left with some ganache, don't waste it, you can use it for truffles; refrigerate the mixture, and once set firm enough, scoop out into small balls and roll in cocoa powder.

Bad Mood Bakes

We all experience changes in our mood – even the most psychologically resilient individuals will experience times of distress, worry, anxiety and gloom. Some of us deal with more persistent episodes, which mean we must dig a little deeper to establish ways to cope with these major shifts in our emotions.

Before I found a real passion for baking, I had started to develop an interest in food, both for its nutritional value and ability to soothe me in times of distress. My go-to creation was a protein ball – I'd blitz together 120g (4oz) super-squidgy dates with a tablespoon of cocoa powder, a tablespoon of protein powder, 60g (2½oz) peanut butter and a sprinkle of chia seeds, then I would meticulously roll the sticky mixture into little balls and store them in the freezer to eat when I fancied. This simple concoction was such a mind-leveller for me – not exactly ground-breaking, but it served a purpose.

Our feelings are personal, of course, and they can be attached to specific events or circumstances, personal health or the health of loved ones, hormone fluctuations, sleep or seasonal changes. Given that low mood comes in different shapes and sizes for everyone, it's sensible to respond to circumstances in an equally personal way.

Sometimes my bad moods are linked to a specific situation. In these cases, they come on quickly and are somewhat volatile, so I need to engage in an activity that will extinguish the wave of emotion. I require a stress-busting bake to help me recalibrate. Bread is my go-to here; it's the perfect antidote to a whirlwind of emotion, with a lengthy kneading session followed by a slow rise and thrilling bake as the dough transforms into bread heaven.

There are other instances that don't have such an easy fix, and it's a case of helping myself through the difficult times as best I can. Baking doesn't necessarily provide the answers, but it can certainly offer a glimmer of light. At times like this, the bakes I seek out are varied: sometimes it'll be something super-simple so nothing can go wrong and destabilize me further, while other times it might serve a nutritional purpose in a bid to keep me physically fit and well. Or I might simply choose something that satisfies me by providing a moment of unrivalled euphoria and revelling in the deliciousness of the end product.

Certain bakes can physically boost our moods, too. Mood can be influenced by myriad factors, so a causal link is difficult to determine, but there is considerable evidence linking certain foods and our brain health. For example, dark chocolate is rich in compounds that may increase feel-good chemicals in our brains; bananas are a source of natural sugar, vitamin B6 and prebiotic fibre, which work together to keep blood sugar levels (and, thereby mood) more stable; oats can stabilize blood sugar levels; and nuts and seeds contain amino acids and minerals that may support brain function.

With all this in mind, the recipes in this chapter aim to have you covered against all manner of dismal days.

Oh-so-moreish Savoury Granola

I've always been a snack fiend. As a kid it was often something savoury like butter and Marmite on milk roll toast, olives, salted nuts, cheese and of course crisps. Nowadays, I've developed a sweet tooth to match my savoury predilection, but when I'm feeling particularly low, I often revert to youth and a salty snack is all I desire. That's where this granola comes in.

There's also something incredibly cathartic about the preparation of granola; it's ridiculously simple and quick to prepare and ready to delve into within the hour. This stuff lasts well, is an excellent salad topper as well as being a reliable snacking companion and is a nutrient powerhouse.

Makes
about 200g (7oz)

Hands-on time
10 minutes

Cooking time
20–25 minutes

Preheat the oven to 180°C/160°C fan/350°F/Gas 4. Line a baking tray with baking parchment.

Combine the oats, spelt flakes, nuts, coconut, seeds, fennel seeds, nigella seeds, chilli flakes and lime zest in a large bowl and stir to combine. In another small bowl, combine the olive oil, soy sauce and maple syrup.

In a separate bowl, whisk the aquafaba or egg white to soft peaks.

Pour the olive oil mixture over the dry ingredients and mix with a spoon or spatula to ensure all of the dry ingredients are evenly coated. Finally, fold through the whipped aquafaba or egg white in two stages.

Pour the mixture onto the baking tray, spread out and bake in the oven for 20–25 minutes, or until crisp and golden – keep an eye on it towards the end of the cooking time as you don't want the nuts to colour too much.

Once baked, remove from the oven and leave to cool on the baking tray. Transfer to a jar and eat as a salad topper or healthy snack.

50g (2oz) jumbo rolled oats

50g (2oz) spelt flakes (or use more oats)

55g (2¼oz) mixed nuts, roughly chopped

2 tbsp coconut chips

55g (2¼oz) mixed seeds (sunflower seeds, pumpkin seeds, linseeds, sesame seeds)

1 tsp fennel seeds

1 tsp nigella seeds

½ tsp chilli flakes (optional)

Zest of ½ lime

10ml (2 tsp) olive oil

10ml (2 tsp) soy sauce

10ml (2 tsp) maple syrup

35ml (1¼fl oz) aquafaba or 1 egg white (see Notes)

Notes

Aquafaba is the liquid drained from a tin of chickpeas. If using egg white instead, reserve the yolk and use it as an egg wash for some Cheese 'n' Spice Scones (see page 172) or for the custard for the Baked Raspberry and Custard Cream Doughnuts (see page 145).

If you fancy varying this recipe, I recommend switching the spices up – use the oats, nuts and seeds as above, but opt for 1 teaspoon each of coriander seeds, cumin seeds, nigella seeds and fennel seeds, ½ teaspoon paprika and a pinch of smoked salt. Choose honey over maple syrup and omit the soy sauce and lime zest.

Lunchbox Muffins

Makes
12 muffins

Hands-on time
20 minutes

Cooking time
20–25 minutes

I always think lunches are awkward. They sit in this no-man's land in the middle of the day, and while they're necessary, they are also a hassle, as you have to break away from what you're doing and, if you haven't had the foresight to prepare something in advance, you end up faced with decisions – and let's be honest, the last thing you want when you're frazzled with work is a decision. In comes the emergency muffin. Bake a batch of these on a Sunday (and obviously snaffle a couple fresh out the oven because they're excellent when still warm), then cool, freeze and defrost from the freezer as and when you need.

Not only do they reduce the psychological burden of the lunch conundrum, but they're also a balanced little meal. There's wholegrains and veggies for carbohydrates and fibre, egg and cheese for protein, some olive oil, seeds and olives for fat, and an array of herbs and lemon zest to elevate the flavour. Freestyle with your ingredients if you don't have those suggested below and thank yourself profusely each time you tuck in for deciding to bake them in the first place.

These muffins are also great as snacks for hungry children, an on-the-go lunchbox option, to accompany soup or served instead of bread for a dinner party.

160ml (5½fl oz) whole milk

10ml (2 tsp) lemon juice

2 large eggs

110ml (3¾fl oz) olive oil (I use a combination of extra virgin and light olive oil)

150g (5oz) self-raising flour

70g (2¾oz) wholemeal flour

½ tsp baking powder

½ tsp bicarbonate of soda

½ heaped tsp sea salt

Pinch of black pepper

1 tsp caster sugar

60g (2½oz) shallot, finely chopped

100g (3½oz) courgette, coarsely grated

100g (3½oz) black olives, finely sliced

120g (4oz) halloumi, cubed

4 tsp dried mint

2 tbsp finely chopped coriander

2 tsp chopped parsley

Zest of 1 lemon

Topping

20g (¾oz) halloumi, finely grated

2 tsp nigella seeds

2 tsp sesame seeds

Preheat the oven to 190°C/170°C fan/375°F/Gas 5. Line a muffin pan with paper cases.

Combine the milk and lemon juice in a small bowl and leave for about 10 minutes to thicken a little.

In a large bowl, lightly whisk the egg, then add the thickened milk mixture and oil and whisk to combine.

In a separate bowl, sift together the flours, baking powder, bicarbonate of soda, salt, pepper and sugar.

Add the dry ingredients to the wet ingredients in two stages, gently whisking with each addition until the mixture is free of lumps. Using a spatula or wooden spoon, gently fold through the shallot, grated courgette, olives, halloumi, mint, coriander, parsley and lemon zest.

Evenly distribute the batter between the muffin cases and sprinkle each one with a pinch of the grated halloumi followed by a sprinkle of nigella and sesame seeds.

Bake for 20–25 minutes, or until a skewer inserted into the centre comes out clean. Once baked, transfer to a wire rack to cool a little before tucking in.

Notes

Halloumi generally comes in 250g (9oz) blocks as standard. You can double up and make 24 muffins instead to make use of all the cheese. Otherwise I like to slice the remaining cheese and cook it under the grill until golden on each side. Serve it with a salad of roasted tomatoes, peppers, courgettes and aubergines. Make a dressing of olive oil, lemon, parsley, mint, salt and pepper and top with some crunchy croutons made from stale bread for a perfect lunch.

You needn't be limited to the flavour combination in the main recipe. Also try:

· Goat's cheese, red onion and rosemary.

· Gruyère, sage and onion.

· Feta, sun-dried tomato, olive and basil.

Wholesome Bread

Makes
1 large loaf

Hands-on time
40 minutes + 4½ hours soaking, resting and proving time

Cooking time
50 minutes

Dough

200g (7oz) wholemeal bread flour, plus extra for dusting

200g (7fl oz) tepid water

1 tbsp malt extract

300g (11oz) strong white bread flour

10g (¼oz) salt

7g (¼oz) sachet of fast-action dried yeast

Seed soaker

30g (1¼oz) pumpkin seeds

30g (1¼oz) sunflower seeds

30g (1¼oz) linseeds

10g (¼oz) sesame seeds

200ml (7fl oz) just-boiled water

Topping (optional)

30g (1¼oz) mixed seeds (a similar mix to above works well)

It's no secret that I love bread, but do you know what else I love? Seeds and nuts! Call me a bird or a squirrel, I don't care, because frankly, I'm a big fan. They're great as they come, but roast them and things get really serious; their flavour is enhanced and they take on a delicate crunch that really adds to the enjoyment. It's no surprise, then, that I'm also a fan of adding seeds to my bread, as they bring a wonderful flavour and texture as well as providing some welcome nutrients.

Here I've teamed a variety of seeds with the extra nuttiness of wholemeal flour – it just so happens that as well as flavour, we're also adding a healthy dose of extra fibre. This recipe requires you to soak roasted seeds, which helps retain moisture in the dough and prevent it from being too heavy. It requires a fair amount of kneading but, generally speaking, it's a pretty simple loaf to prepare. You could feasibly start this in the early morning and have it ready for lunch… just my kind of bread bake! Serve buttered with soup or piled with your favourite sandwich filling, or slice and freeze leftovers for wonderful toast in the coming days.

Preheat the oven to 200°C/180°C fan/400°F/Gas 6. Spread the seeds for the seed soaker onto a baking tray and bake for 10 minutes, or until golden and aromatic. Set aside and allow to cool.

Meanwhile, sift the wholemeal flour into a large bowl – you should be left with the bran part of the flour in the sieve. Transfer the bran to a medium heatproof bowl, add the cooled seeds and mix to combine. Pour over the just-boiled water and leave to soak for a minimum of 1 hour.

Measure out the tepid water into a large jug and add the malt extract, stirring to dissolve. Add the white bread flour to the sifted wholewheat flour, then add the salt and yeast to different sides of the bowl. Add the seed soaker and the malt mixture and bring together to form a shaggy dough. Cover and leave to rest at room temperature for 20 minutes.

Once rested, knead the dough for 10 minutes, either by hand or in a stand mixer, then cover again and rest for a further 10 minutes, before kneading for a final 5 minutes, or until stretchy and noticeably smooth.

Note

You can use a baking tray instead of a cast-iron pan. Place a heatproof tray in the bottom of the oven as well. Transfer the loaf and parchment to the preheated tray, return it to the oven and pour a cup of water into the tray in the bottom (this will generate steam to create a nice crust). Bake as below.

Cover again and leave to prove somewhere warm for 1–2 hours, or until doubled in size.

Once rested, turn the dough out onto a very lightly floured surface. Imagining the dough is a compass, gently stretch the west side point up and over to the centre, then repeat with the east side. Next, gently stretch the north side point up and over to the centre before repeating with the south side. You should have created a parcel. Flip the dough over and, keeping your hands in contact with the work surface, cup the dough from the furthest side away from you and drag it towards you a little, then rotate the dough 90 degrees and repeat until you form a nice taut, round ball of dough.

Once shaped, transfer to a medium bowl lined with a floured tea towel, cover and leave to prove for 1 hour, or until noticeably risen, soft and when poked, it springs back slowly.

Around 30 minutes before you intend to bake, place a lidded cast-iron pan in the oven and preheat the oven to 245°C/225°C fan/475°F/Gas 9.

Once the loaf has proved and the oven is nice and hot, remove the cast-iron pan from the oven and take off the lid. Turn out the loaf onto a piece of baking parchment and use a sharp knife or lame to score the loaf with four slashes to make a square shape on top. Sprinkle the top of the dough with seeds. Use the parchment under the dough to carefully transfer and lower the loaf into the pan.

Replace the lid and bake in the oven for 30 minutes before removing the lid and continuing to bake for a further 15–20 minutes, or until a deep golden brown and sounding hollow when tapped on the base.

Once baked, remove from the oven and allow to cool fully on a wire rack before you tuck in.

Flax and Oat Rolls

Bread baking has repeatedly been recognized for its therapeutic benefits. Bread was my route into baking, partly through a passion for the stuff and a desire for quality that I couldn't find elsewhere, but also through intrigue. How could such humble ingredients yield something quite so delicious? I later found that I had to be patient, too (something I'm terrible at), I had to engage both my hands and my brain, and the anticipation of the outcome was a real thrill. It sounds cliché, but it was a truly immersive experience.

It goes without saying, then, that a decent bread-baking session can release a lot of a tension for me. It really helps to silence negative brain chatter by diverting my attention. These rolls require a decent amount of kneading, one of the best methods for relieving pent-up stress or frustration, and they're packed with fibre but still incredibly light and fluffy when baked, so the eating experience is as comforting as the process. They're the perfect soft dinner roll, served with a smear of salted butter, or as a vehicle for an epic sandwich or burger.

Makes
12 rolls

Hands-on time
30 minutes + 3½ hours proving time

Cooking time
20–25 minutes

240g (8½oz) strong white bread flour

115g (4oz) wholemeal bread flour

45g (1¾oz) rolled oats

40g (1½oz) ground flaxseed

10g (¼oz) fast-action dried yeast

8g (1½ tsp) sea salt

60g (2½oz) runny honey (I use acacia honey)

50g (2oz) rapeseed or olive oil (rapeseed gives a more buttery flavour)

60ml (2½fl oz) orange juice

200ml (7fl oz) lukewarm water

50ml (2fl oz) water or milk, for brushing

50g (2oz) mixed seeds

Combine the flours, oats and flaxseed in a large bowl or the bowl of a stand mixer and stir to combine. Add the yeast to one side of the bowl and the salt to the other.

In a large jug, combine the honey, oil, orange juice and water and stir briefly to combine before adding to the dry ingredients (ensure you have added all the honey as it tends to stick to the bottom of the jug). Mix gently and bring the ingredients together into a soft, shaggy dough. Knead for 8–10 minutes, either on a lightly oiled surface or in a mixer on medium speed, then cover the dough with a damp tea towel and leave to rest for 10 minutes.

Once rested, knead for a further 8–10 minutes, or until smooth and elastic. Place in a lightly oiled bowl, cover and prove in a warm place for 1½–2 hours, or until doubled in size.

Once proved, remove the dough from the bowl and divide into approximately 12 equally sized pieces. Use your hand to roll into tight, round balls before transferring to a baking tray lined with baking parchment. Leave a small gap between each ball to allow for them to expand during the second prove – they will touch during this time, which is fine. Cover a second time and leave to prove in a warm place for another 1½ hours, or until almost doubled in size.

Twenty minutes prior to baking, preheat the oven to 180°C/160°C fan/350°F/Gas 4. When the rolls are nicely risen, brush them with water or milk (you won't need it all), and sprinkle with seeds of your choice. Bake in the oven for 20–25 minutes, or until golden brown. Once baked, remove from the oven and gently transfer to a wire rack to cool.

Enjoy with burgers, a comforting soup or filled with your favourite sandwich filling.

Pick 'n' Mix Florentines

Florentines remind me of Christmas day; that moment when you've finished your roast, shovelled in some dessert (always including brandy sauce, because I live for that stuff at Christmas) and you retire to the living room with a (decaf) coffee or something stronger and a snack. In our house, the snack that emerges is a Florentine. You're stuffed, yet you can always make room for one of these little devils. They are the ultimate biscuit-chocolate fusion – nuts bound by caramel, studded with dried fruit and coated in chocolate. This recipe captures the perfect balance between chewy and crunchy, in my opinion, jewelled with plump fruit and smeared with a thin layer of chocolate. I've provided a few flavour combinations to suit different preferences, so use the caramel and nut and seed base recipes paired with one of the three flavour combinations.

Makes
16–18

Hands-on time
15 minutes

Cooking time
about 10–12 minutes
+ 20 minutes
cooling time

Caramel

50ml (2fl oz) double cream

15g (½oz) unsalted butter

50g (2oz) golden syrup

60g (2½oz) soft light brown sugar

Nut and seed base

90g (3¼oz) toasted flaked almonds

10g (¼oz) sesame seeds

15g (½oz) toasted coconut chips

10g (¼oz) cornflakes, crushed

¼ tsp sea salt

Cherry, pistachio and ginger with dark chocolate

20g (¾oz) slivered pistachios

45g (1¾oz) dried cherries, roughly chopped

15g (½oz) crystallized ginger, roughly chopped

150g (5oz) 75% dark chocolate, roughly chopped

Salted caramel, toasted hazelnut and milk chocolate

20g (¾oz) hazelnuts, toasted and halved

45g (1¾oz) flame raisins, roughly chopped

150g (5oz) milk chocolate, roughly chopped

Cranberry, orange and white chocolate

20g (¾oz) whole almonds, toasted and chopped

25g (1oz) dried cranberries, roughly chopped

20g (¾oz) candied orange peel, roughly chopped

150g (5oz) white or caramelized white chocolate, roughly chopped

Preheat the oven to 180°C/160°C fan/350°F/Gas 4 and line a baking tray with baking parchment.

First make the nut and seed base. Combine all the ingredients in a large bowl, and then add the additional nuts from the flavour combination you have chosen (pistachios, hazelnuts or whole almonds). Mix together.

Next make the caramel. In a small saucepan, combine the cream, butter, golden syrup and soft light brown sugar. Place over a low heat and stir to combine, allowing the sugar to dissolve before increasing the heat and bringing the mixture to the boil. Once boiling, remove from the heat and pour over the seed and nut mixture. Stir well to ensure that the dry ingredients are evenly coated. Allow to cool for 5 minutes, then stir again to redistribute any syrup that has sunk to the bottom of the bowl.

Scoop out 15–20g (½–¾oz) spoonfuls of the mixture and dollop onto the baking tray, spaced well apart (they spread a lot). Once all the mixture has been used up, bake in the oven for 8–10 minutes until part-baked and golden, then remove from the oven.

If the Florentine mixture has spread everywhere, use a greased spatula to nudge each portion back into an approximate circle. Carefully sprinkle over your chosen chopped dried fruits, distributing them as evenly as possible – use the spatula to nudge them in properly, don't get your fingers too close to the hot caramel! Return to the oven for 2 minutes. Keep an eye on them to make sure the fruit and caramel don't burn.

Once baked, remove from the oven, and, working relatively quickly, use a lightly greased round cookie cutter to nudge each Florentine into a neat circular shape. Leave to cool on the tray.

Meanwhile, melt your chosen chocolate in the microwave or in a heatproof bowl placed over a pan of gently simmering water. Once the Florentines have cooled, dip the flat sides into the chocolate. Allow any excess to drip off and use a palette knife to neaten. Repeat with all the Florentines, then cool on a wire rack or plate until set firm. You can also help them set by popping them in the fridge for about 15 minutes.

Notes

Tempered chocolate is the name given to chocolate that has been melted and cooled in a stable manner to achieve a wonderful shine and that all-important 'snap'.

A relatively basic tempering technique is to very slowly melt four-fifths of the chocolate, then, once melted, add the remaining chocolate, finely chopped, and keep stirring with a spatula until it is smooth, glossy and a little thicker – you're aiming for a temperature of 29°C (84°F) for dark chocolate and 28°C (82°F) for milk or white chocolate on a digital thermometer.

However, tempering chocolate is difficult and a faff – I think I have achieved it a handful of times, mainly by accident – so I'm inclined to suggest we leave that wizardry to the skilled pastry chefs out there.

Vegan Cinnamon Pretzel Bites

I must have lived a fairly sheltered life because my first introduction to baked pretzels (not the savoury snack you eat like crisps) was not until the grand age of 18. By this point in my life, I had started to form a difficult relationship with food. I no longer saw it as a pleasure, nor did I acknowledge its role in fuelling my body; I saw it as something to be controlled and 'perfected', while the rest of my life felt in disarray.

It's unsurprising, then, that when I finally mustered up the courage to sample a warm, pillowy soft and chewy cinnamon sugar pretzel on a trip to London, I was whisked off to a place of food-induced nirvana. This warm, baked snack, cocooned in its crumpled paper bag, became embedded in my memory... and therefore continues to be something I marvel at. I have taken to my little home test kitchen to replicate that feeling, avoiding the faff of shaping the pretzels by resorting to simple bite-size chunks (this also means more surface area for the cinnamon sugar to adhere to). The dough incorporates a pre-formed roux called a tangzhong, which helps to generate that tender texture.

Makes
around 40 pretzel bites

Hands-on time
30 minutes + 2½ hours proving and resting time

Cooking time
10 minutes

Tangzhong

20g (¾oz) strong white bread flour

100ml (3½fl oz) water

Dough

300g (11oz) strong white bread flour

7 cardamom pods, bashed open and seeds finely ground

7g (¼oz) sachet of fast-action dried yeast

5g (1 tsp) sea salt

20g (¾oz) malt extract

140ml (4¾fl oz) dairy-free milk (I like soya but almond and oat also work well)

40ml (1½fl oz) olive oil

Bicarbonate of soda solution

2 tbsp bicarbonate of soda

250ml (8fl oz) just-boiled water

Cinnamon sugar dip

30g (1¼oz) vegan butter

1½ tbsp ground cinnamon

100g (3½oz) caster sugar

First prepare the tangzhong. Combine the flour and water in a saucepan and whisk gently until no lumps remain. Place over a medium heat and cook for 1–3 minutes, stirring regularly, until thickened and resembling a thick paste. Remove from the heat and transfer to a bowl to cool.

Meanwhile, combine the flour, ground cardamom, yeast and salt in a large bowl, keeping the salt and yeast on opposite sides of the bowl. Once the tangzhong has cooled completely, add to the dry ingredients along with the malt extract, milk and olive oil. Mix by hand or on a low speed in a stand mixer with the dough hook attachment.

Once the dough has come together, knead it for 10–15 minutes until it is smooth and very elastic (a 10–20 minute rest between forming the dough and kneading can make the dough more manageable if you are working by hand). Transfer the dough to a lightly oiled bowl, cover and leave to prove in a warm place for around 1½ –2 hours.

Preheat the oven to 200°C/180°C fan/400°F/Gas 6. Line two large baking trays with baking parchment.

Once the dough has risen, remove it from the bowl and divide into eight pieces. Roll the each piece into ropes about 20–24cm (8–9½in) in length. Cut each rope into around five chunks and place on the baking tray. Leave to rest, covered with a damp tea towel, for 30 minutes.

Meanwhile, prepare the bicarbonate of soda solution. Combine the water and bicarbonate of soda, stirring until the soda is totally dissolved. Set the mixture aside to cool to a lukewarm temperature.

Once the dough chunks have rested, dip each one into the warm bicarbonate of soda solution for around 10 seconds before transferring back to the baking tray. Bake for 10 minutes, or until golden brown.

While the pretzel bites bake, prepare the cinnamon sugar dip. Melt the vegan butter and combine the sugar and cinnamon in a separate bowl.

Once baked, remove the bites from the oven, brush each bite with butter, then roll in the cinnamon sugar before placing on a wire rack to cool. Serve warm.

Notes

To make these savoury – and therefore an excellent accompaniment to dinner party dips – scale down the malt extract in the dough to 10g (¼oz) and make as instructed, omitting the cinnamon sugar and instead sprinkling with a little flaky sea salt. Alternatively, scatter over some grated Cheddar or Gruyère prior to baking to create little cheesy morsels of heaven.

If you are partial to a bit of chocolate in your life, you could whip up a simple dipping sauce once the pretzels are baked. Combine 200g (7oz) milk or dark chocolate, 100g (3½oz) double cream, 100ml (3½fl oz) whole milk and 60g (2½oz) golden syrup with a hefty pinch of salt in a saucepan. Place over a low heat and gently melt together. Once you have a smooth shiny sauce, remove from the heat and transfer to a jug or serving bowl. Dip, dip, dip away!

This recipe makes more cinnamon sugar than you will need, but I like to reserve the excess to sprinkle on porridge or baked apples.

Spiced Root Veg Traybake

Imagine a cake full of fruit and veg? Are you green at the thought? It sounds grim, I know, but somehow, this cake just works. Absolutely packed full of fibre and healthy fats, it's verging on 'nutritious' and is remarkably uncompromised as a result.

When I'm feeling particularly low, or irritable, I'm not especially good at concentrating, yet consuming myself in a bake is a dependable form of therapy. In this instance, a recipe like this really delivers; simple in terms of construction but engaging enough due to the number of ingredients to prepare.

It's very reminiscent of a carrot cake in terms of flavour and texture; nutty, fruity, 'moist', and super-spiced, wonderfully comforting to consume and, if you're prepared to share a square or two, a real crowd-pleaser.

Makes
16 squares

Hands-on time
35 minutes + 1 hour soaking time

Cooking time
45 minutes

Preheat the oven to 180°C/160°C fan/350°F/Gas 4. Grease a 20 x 20cm (8 x 8in) square tin and line with baking parchment.

Combine the sultanas with the orange zest and juice in a small bowl and leave to soak for approximately 1 hour.

Pour the oil into a large jug, add the eggs and whisk to combine. Sift the two flours into a separate bowl and add the baking powder, bicarbonate of soda, cinnamon and mixed spice. Add the sugar and mix well.

Next, add the sultana and orange juice mixture, grated vegetables, walnuts and egg mixture and mix thoroughly with a spatula.

Once all of the ingredients are fully incorporated, pour the batter into the prepared tin and bake in the oven for about 40 minutes, or until a skewer inserted into the centre of the cake comes out clean and it's shrinking away from the sides of the tin. Once cooked, leave for 5 minutes in the tin before turning out onto a wire rack to cool.

Meanwhile, prepare the frosting. Combine the cream cheese, Greek yoghurt, icing sugar and lemon zest in a bowl – don't overbeat or the mixture will end up too loose.

Once the cake has fully cooled, swirl the frosting over the cake before carefully cutting it into 16 equal portions (it can be a little fragile, but I find that the more fragile the cake, the better it tastes!).

Decorate each square with more toasted nuts, a sprig of rosemary and a pinch of cinnamon, if you wish. Pop the kettle on, sit back and enjoy!

50g (2oz) sultanas

Zest of 1 orange, plus 50ml (2fl oz) juice

125g (4¼oz) grapeseed oil

2 large eggs

85g (3oz) wholemeal flour

85g (3oz) self-raising flour

1 tsp baking powder

1 tsp bicarbonate of soda

2 tsp ground cinnamon

2 tsp ground mixed spice

140g (4¾oz) light brown muscovado sugar

210g (7¼oz) finely grated mixed carrot, parsnip and beetroot (about 1 medium carrot, 1 small beetroot and ½ parsnip)

50g (2oz) walnuts, toasted and finely chopped, plus walnut halves to decorate

Frosting and decoration

100g (3½oz) cream cheese

100g (3½oz) full-fat Greek yoghurt (use a thick, set yoghurt such as Fage)

25g (1oz) icing sugar

½ tsp finely grated lemon zest

Rosemary sprigs, to decorate (optional)

Ground cinnamon, for sprinkling (optional)

Caribbean Banana Bread

The sight of a banana bread recipe may have you rolling your eyes. How can there be yet another version of the same concept? I'd probably think the same myself... but here is my defence: firstly, during lockdown, I learned that bananas are one of the most wasted food products, and for someone who hates waste and loves bananas, this makes me very sad. Secondly, I never settle on one version of something being the best, which means I try endless recipes, build on my knowledge and work towards my version of perfection. Thirdly, this recipe is laced with wholesome ingredients and is the epitome of a great cut-and-come-again cake, improving on day two, three and even four. A slice of this fragrant, moist banana bread is perfect served to guests with tea or popped under the grill, lightly toasted and buttered for a scrumptious weekend breakfast.

Serves
10–12

Hands-on time
15 minutes

Cooking time
50–60 minutes

~~~~~~

300g (11oz) ripe banana flesh (about 3 medium bananas)

1 tsp dark rum (optional)

80g (3oz) wholemeal flour, sifted

50g (2oz) spelt flour, sifted

80g (3oz) plain flour, sifted

¼ tsp sea salt

1 tsp baking powder

1 tsp bicarbonate of soda

⅛ tsp ground cloves

2 tsp ground cinnamon

75g (2¾oz) sour cream

2 large eggs

65ml (2½fl oz) maple syrup

100g (3½oz) soft light brown sugar

1 tsp vanilla extract

100g (3½oz) coconut oil, melted and cooled slightly

10–15g (¼–½oz) cold unsalted butter, cut into matchsticks

Note

Try adding 50–75g (2–2¾oz) lightly toasted chopped walnuts for an earthy tang or some dark chocolate chips – banana/coconut/chocolate, need I say more?

Preheat the oven to 180°C/160°C fan/350°F/Gas 4 and line a 900g (2lb) loaf tin with baking parchment.

Mash the bananas in a large bowl, add the rum, if using, and set aside while you prepare the other ingredients.

In a separate bowl, combine the sifted flours, salt, baking powder, bicarbonate of soda, ground cloves and 1 teaspoon of the cinnamon.

Combine the sour cream, eggs, maple syrup, sugar and vanilla extract in a medium bowl and pour in the coconut oil, then add to the mashed banana. Now add the dry ingredients to the wet ingredients and fold through, but don't overmix the batter.

Transfer to the prepared loaf tin. Sprinkle the remaining teaspoon of cinnamon over the top of the cake batter, using a cocktail stick or skewer to swirl it around for a cinnamon 'ripple'.

For the perfect crack in the top of your banana bread, carefully position the cold butter matchsticks on top of the batter in a line down the centre. Bake in the oven for 50–60 minutes, or until a skewer inserted into the cake comes out clean.

Allow to cool in the tin for 15–20 minutes before carefully removing and leaving to cool completely on a wire rack. It is delicious served on the day of baking but improves by the next day.

Passion Fruit and Dark Chocolate Profiteroles

Makes
14 profiteroles

Hands-on time
30 minutes

Cooking time
30 minutes

Choux pastry defies logic; you create a sticky paste-like batter that is beaten to oblivion, and when baked, it puffs up like delicate, tender, lighter-than-air clouds – complete wizardry! Eaten alone, choux pastry can be a little underwhelming, but when paired with a creamy, fruity, rich filling and dunked (or, frankly, drowned) in chocolate, it's pure joy! I've kept things fairly traditional by filling my choux buns with cream and topping them with a silky chocolate ganache, with an extra element of sophistication from tangy passion fruit curd, which is both nestled beneath the cream and infused in the ganache. Think of them as sort of 'grown-up' profiteroles.

60ml (2½fl oz) semi-skimmed milk

60g (2½oz) unsalted butter

60ml (2½fl oz) water

¼ tsp sea salt

½ tsp caster sugar

65g (2½oz) strong white bread flour, sifted

100–110g (3½–3¾oz) lightly beaten egg (about 2 large eggs)

Filling

250ml (8fl oz) double cream

180g (6¼oz) Passion Fruit Curd (see page 183)

Passion fruit chocolate ganache

100g (3½oz) dark chocolate

10g (¼oz) golden syrup

10g (¼oz) unsalted butter

55ml (2¼oz) double cream

20ml (4 tsp) strained passion fruit juice (from about 2 passion fruit)

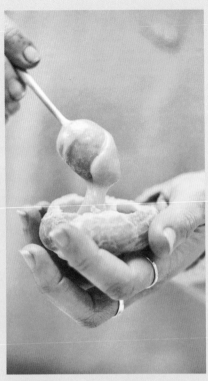

Note

This recipe is a great use for any leftover passion fruit curd from the Tropical Coconut, Passion Fruit and Rum Cake recipe (see page 183), but it can also be a canvas for your imagination to run wild – think cherry jam and kirsch Chantilly cream topped with chocolate ganache for a Black Forest vibe, or salted caramel and coffee cream topped with chocolate ganache for a mocha version.

Preheat the oven to 220°C/200°C fan/425°F/Gas 7 and line two baking trays with baking parchment.

Combine the milk, butter, water, salt and sugar in a medium saucepan over a low heat and allow the butter to melt, stirring occasionally. Once melted, increase the heat and bring to the boil. Take the pan off the heat and quickly add the sifted flour, beating vigorously with a wooden spoon until a smooth dough forms. Place back over a low heat and continue to stir for 1–2 minutes until the mixture starts to dry out and pull away from the sides of the pan – a dry film will form on the base of the pan.

Transfer the dough to a large heatproof bowl and allow to cool for 1–2 minutes. Add the lightly beaten eggs to the dough in a few stages, beating thoroughly between each addition – don't worry if it looks curdled at first, it will come back together as you beat. Continue to add the egg until the mixture reaches dropping consistency and is shiny – you may not need all of the egg.

Transfer the dough to a piping bag fitted with a large round nozzle and pipe 4cm (1½in) rounds onto the lined baking trays, smoothing any peaks with a damp finger.

Bake in the oven for 15 minutes, then turn the temperature down to 185°C/165°C fan/350°F/Gas 4 and bake for a further 10–15 minutes, or until puffed up and golden brown. Once baked, remove from the oven and pierce the side of each profiterole with the tip of a large knife or a skewer to allow the steam to escape. Transfer to a wire rack to cool.

Prepare the cream by beating to medium soft peaks. Refrigerate until ready to use.

For the ganache, melt the chocolate, golden syrup and butter in a heatproof bowl over a pan of gently simmering water. Combine the cream with the strained passion fruit juice in a jug. Remove the melted chocolate from the heat and stir in the cream. Cool for 10–15 minutes.

To assemble, cut the profiteroles horizontally through the middle and fill the bases with a heaped teaspoon of passion fruit curd. Transfer the whipped cream to a piping bag and pipe a neat swirl over the passion fruit curd. Dip the 'lids' of the profiteroles in the ganache, allowing any excess to neatly drip off, and carefully place over the filled bases. Once assembled, serve within a couple of hours or refrigerate – the pastry will soften but they will still have all the same charm the next day.

Banana and Peanut Choc-ice Bites

I felt like a bit of a fraud including this recipe in the book due to its relative simplicity. However, it struck me that often we get far more joy, peace and happiness from the simple things in life. Some of the most comforting bakes – shortbread, flapjacks, a soft white sandwich loaf – remain favourites despite the invention of more elaborate concepts.

This recipe is the ultimate mood booster; it is the perfect union of sweet, salty, nutty and bitter flavours and the simple process is incredibly mentally absorbing. Better still, these humble ingredients have been recognized for their ability to enhance mental well-being. Obviously, these little bites are a winner in the summer months, but if you're anything like me, they'll be on the menu year-round as a perfect little pick-me-up.

Makes
10–15

Hands-on time
20 minutes + 3 hours freezing time

Arrange the banana slices on a baking tray lined with baking parchment. Spread each banana disc with ½ teaspoon of peanut butter, or enough to cover the surface, then transfer to the freezer for 1 hour to firm up.

Put the chocolate into a heatproof bowl and place over a saucepan containing 2.5cm (1in) gently simmering water. Slowly melt the chocolate, stirring occasionally. Once almost melted, whisk in the oil and continue to stir until you have a glossy molten mixture.

Arrange your desired toppings in ramekins on the work surface and line a second baking tray with baking parchment.

Retrieve the bananas from the freezer. Use a spoon to dip each disc into the chocolate, coating it all over. Quickly remove it (you don't want the chocolate to be too thick) and place on the second baking tray. Sprinkle with your chosen decoration. Repeat with the remaining banana discs.

Once all the discs are coated and decorated, return the tray to the freezer for 1–2 hours to set hard. Transfer to an airtight container and store in the freezer for up to a month to grab in times of need!

1 large or 2 small ripe bananas, peeled and sliced into 1cm (½in) discs

50g (2oz) smooth or crunchy peanut butter

Coating

100g (3½oz) dark or milk chocolate, roughly chopped

10g (2 tsp) coconut or vegetable oil

Decoration

Desiccated coconut

Freeze-dried raspberries

Slivered pistachios, peanuts, almonds or hazelnuts

Flaky sea salt (optional)

Time to Unwind

Many people turn to baking to help them unwind. In today's society, speed seems to be rewarded, be it through career promotions, praise from peers, 'winning' a timed competition, or just our personal belief that we've done something well if we've done it quickly. We fill our days and weeks with activities and jobs and rush to get them done; we strive to squeeze in just a bit more of everything to enhance our feeling of accomplishment.

Ironically, this desire to get more done more quickly doesn't make us more efficient – in fact, we end up stressed, anxious and exhausted, we don't pay enough attention to tasks, we underperform and sometimes we let people down as a result. The consequence of this is that our mental health can suffer, either because we are not looking after ourselves physically (and therefore mentally), or because a drop in our performance makes us feel like a failure – we continually perceive others to be doing things better and quicker than us, and thereby feel inadequate. What's more, relationships may become compromised, which can lead to isolation.

Slowing down is therefore fundamental to supporting ourselves both psychologically and physically. Many of the processes involved in baking are a perfect solution to our tendency to stress and fuss over things. The physical and immersive act of measuring and combining ingredients forces us to focus our attention on the senses, tuning in to sights, sounds and smells. We are often at the mercy of science when baking – allowing dough to prove, resting pastry, chilling cake batter, baking low and slow. As we are forced to slow down, we gain a heightened sense of awareness; we are rewarded with feelings of calm and clarity, which, applied to other aspects of life, can often result in greater success. This significant drop in pace gives us better control over our thoughts, and our emotions are given a chance to stabilize.

The act of baking is mindful and meditative, providing an immediate form of stress relief and a way to escape the treadmill of life. So, in this chapter I've included everything from sweet dough buns that are slowly kneaded before you can watch them rise magically, to delicately handled rough puff pastry with tender, flaky layers, and fluffy meringues, baked slowly for the ultimate soft centre and delicate outer shell. These recipes take some time, but don't be deterred: the psychological reward and gratifying outcome will have you coming back for more. As ever, I suggest ways in which the recipes can be altered to suit the season, your taste or your mood at any given moment; I encourage you to listen to your body and be the master of your bake, as this will undoubtedly provide the greatest psychological benefit and personal satisfaction.

Leek, Mushroom and Cavolo Nero Tart

Serves
6–8

Hands-on time
40 minutes + 4½ hours
resting time

Cooking time
1½ hours

Savoury tarts are majorly overshadowed these days. From pasties, pizza and falafel wraps to loaded sandwiches, soups and superfood salads – convenience, speed and quick-hit satisfaction is so often the preference, especially at lunch. While I'm in favour of all the above, I firmly believe that good old tarts deserve more recognition; a buttery short pastry case filled with silky custard and packed with flavoursome fillings, what more could you want? Of course, this isn't a quick-fix bake – it's somewhat a labour of love; baking in layers, one might say. But this uncomplicated, slow and peaceful process yields unrivalled calm.

I've opted for leek, mushroom and cavolo nero to generously fill this tart. The leeks and mushrooms are given a lengthy sauté to intensify their flavours and the briefly blanched cavolo nero offers a little robustness in texture as well as a delicate, earthy flavour to complement the sweet unctuousness of the leek and mushroom. Finally, a hefty sprinkle of Cheddar cheese adds more flavour, as well as a lovely browned top for the tart. This is a Sunday bake at its best, with leftovers for lunches throughout the week.

Pastry

200g (7oz) plain flour

50g (2oz) rye flour

150g (5oz) cold unsalted butter, cubed

50ml (2fl oz) ice-cold water

½ tsp white wine vinegar

½ large egg, beaten (use the rest for the custard)

Vegetable filling

15g (½oz) unsalted butter

2 tsp olive oil

2–3 leeks, trimmed, cleaned and sliced

250g (9oz) portobello mushrooms, sliced

50g (2oz) cavolo nero or other kale

90g (3¼oz) extra-mature Cheddar, grated

Sea salt and black pepper

Custard

2½ large eggs, beaten

110g (3¾oz) sour cream

110ml (3¾fl oz) whipping cream

First prepare the pastry. Put the flours into a food processor and briefly pulse to combine. Add the butter and pulse again until the mixture resembles fine breadcrumbs. Add the ice-cold water and vinegar and pulse until just clumping together, then tip out onto a large square of cling film and use the cling film to gently flatten the pastry into a disc. Rest the pastry in the fridge for at least 4 hours.

Once rested, roll out the pastry to about 3mm (⅛in) thick and gently transfer it to a 20cm (8in) fluted tart tin, pressing the pastry into the sides with the side of your finger. Return to the fridge and chill for at least another 30 minutes.

Meanwhile, prepare the filling. Heat the butter and oil in a large saucepan over a medium heat and add the leeks. Cook for 10 minutes, or until softened. Stir in the mushrooms and cook gently, stirring, for 40 minutes, or until all the moisture has evaporated.

Blanch the cavolo nero in boiling salted water for 1 minute before draining thoroughly. Squeeze out as much excess water as you can and finely chop. Set aside.

Once the leek and mushroom mixture is cooked, turn off the heat, season with salt and pepper to taste and set aside.

Preheat the oven to 200°C/180°C fan/400°F/Gas 6. Line the pastry case with a piece of scrunched up parchment and weigh down with baking beans or uncooked rice.

Bake for 20 minutes, then remove the baking beans and parchment, lightly brush with the beaten egg and return to the oven to bake for a further 5–10 minutes, or until golden brown. Remove from the oven and allow to cool in the tin.

Meanwhile, prepare the custard. Combine all the ingredients in a bowl and beat together until smooth. Pass the liquid mixture through a sieve into a large jug, season and refrigerate until ready to use.

Once everything is prepared, sprinkle the cavolo nero over the base, then spoon in the leek and mushroom mixture. Slowly pour over the custard, filling the pastry as full as you can, then sprinkle over the grated Cheddar. Bake in the oven for 35 minutes, or until puffed up and golden on top.

Notes

Some alternative flavour combinations that I really rate include:

- Roasted vegetables, feta, basil or dill and pine nuts.

- Pea, mint and goat's cheese.

- Spinach, ricotta, nutmeg and Parmesan.

Mini Spanakopita Rolls

My good friend Sally introduced me to spanakopita, a Greek savoury spinach pie flavoured with salty feta, tons of herbs and a little nutmeg and lemon. Traditionally, this flavourful filling is wrapped in layers of buttery filo pastry, however, I've opted for a wonderfully rich flaky pastry that I think complements the filling beautifully. These mini veggie rolls can be served as dinner party canapés or weekend lunches, and leftovers are great the next day in your lunchbox.

Makes
12–15 rolls

Hands-on time
45 minutes + 2 hours chilling time

Cooking time
25–30 minutes

Pastry

200g (7oz) plain flour

160g (5½oz) cold unsalted butter, cubed

½ tsp salt

95g (3¼oz) cold sour cream or buttermilk

Filling

525g (1lb 3oz) fresh spinach (or 450g/1lb frozen spinach, defrosted)

6 spring onions, trimmed and finely sliced

180g (6¼oz) feta, crumbled

15g (½oz) dill, finely chopped

15g (½oz) mint, leaves finely chopped

Zest of 1 lemon

About ⅓ of a whole nutmeg, grated

1 large egg, beaten

3 tbsp fresh breadcrumbs

Sea salt and black pepper

To finish

1 large egg yolk, beaten

1½ tsp sesame seeds

1½ tsp fennel seeds

Combine the flour, butter and salt in a bowl. Rub and press the butter into the flour until the mixture resembles coarse breadcrumbs with a few larger lumps and some flat flakes of butter remaining.

Add the sour cream or buttermilk and use a fork to bring the mixture together into a shaggy dough – it is important not to overwork the dough at this point. Tip the dough out onto a large square of cling film and use the cling film to bring the dough together. Chill for 30 minutes.

Remove the dough from the fridge and roll it into a rectangle about 40 x 15cm (16 x 6in). Starting at one of the shorter edges, fold the top half of the dough into the centre, then fold the bottom half into the centre as well, and finally fold the two halves over one another. This is a double fold. Rotate the dough a quarter turn and repeat, rolling it back out and folding as before. Wrap in cling film and chill for a further 30 minutes.

After this time, take the dough back out and lay it on the work surface with the open seams facing towards you, then roll the dough out for its final double fold and refrigerate again for at least 1 hour.

Meanwhile, prepare the filling. Place the spinach in a sieve and pour over boiling water. Allow to cool, then place it in a muslin cloth (or a clean tea towel) to squeeze out as much moisture as possible. Place in a bowl with the remaining ingredients, season to taste and mix well to combine. Refrigerate until ready to use.

Preheat the oven to 210°C/190°C fan/400°F/Gas 6. Roll the dough out into a rectangle about 15 x 60cm (6 x 24in) and about 3mm (⅛in) thick. Place the filling in a line along one of the longer edges of the dough, 1cm (½in) from the edge, as if you were making a sausage roll.

Use some of the beaten egg yolk to brush the exposed 1cm (½in) of dough. Fold the pastry over the filling and seal. Trim off any excess dough from the ends and cut into 12–15 equal rolls.

Brush the top of the pastry with more of the beaten egg yolk, sprinkle with the sesame and fennel seeds and bake for 25–30 minutes, or until golden brown.

Notes

See page 121 for some ideas on how to use up your pastry scraps.

If you don't have time to make your own pastry for this recipe, shop-bought puff pastry would work (almost) as well.

Hot 'Happy' Buns

I consider myself a pretty 'cup-half-empty' person (I'm not proud of it, but it's a reality) so in the spirit of upping my positivity game, these buns, traditionally referred to as 'cross' are now 'happy' – all swirls and hearts, please!

You probably think I'm selling you yet another standard hot cross bun here – and actually, I kind of am – but hear me out. I've trialled endless hot cross bun recipes over the past few years and have encountered all the potential pitfalls, so it only seems fair to share my findings and hopefully save you from the same hardship. Humming with spice, studded with dried fruit and pillowy soft, these are best eaten still warm from the oven, accompanied by a hefty smear of butter.

Makes
9 small buns

Hands-on time
35 minutes + 3½ hours
proving time

Cooking time
20 minutes

250g (9oz) strong white bread flour, plus extra for dusting

10g (¼oz) golden caster sugar

½ tsp ground cinnamon

¼ tsp ground cardamom

½ tsp ground mixed spice

Zest of ½ orange

Zest of ½ lemon

5g (1 tsp) sea salt

5g (1 tsp) fast-action dried yeast

30g (1¼oz) soft unsalted butter, cubed

30g (1¼oz) runny honey

30g (1¼oz) egg (about ½ large egg)

55g (2¼oz) sultanas, soaked in boiling water for 10 minutes

25g (1oz) mixed peel

Vegetable oil, for greasing

Spice-infused milk

150ml (5fl oz) whole milk

½ cinnamon stick

3 cardamom pods

1 whole nutmeg

Glaze

75g (2¾oz) caster sugar

75g (2¾oz) water

1 tsp honey

1 star anise

1 cinnamon stick

3 cardamom pods

Piping paste

50g (2oz) plain flour

1 tsp caster sugar

40–45ml (1½–1¾fl oz) water

First make the spice-infused milk. Pour the milk into a small saucepan over a medium heat and bring almost to the boil (85°C/185°F on a digital thermometer). Remove from the heat, add the spices and set aside to infuse for around 10 minutes while you prepare the dough.

Combine the flour, caster sugar, cinnamon, cardamom and mixed spice in a large bowl or the bowl of a stand mixer. Briefly mix to combine, then add the orange and lemon zest and give it another quick mix. Next add the salt to one side of the bowl and the yeast to the other.

Remove the whole spices from the infused milk and add the cubed butter along with the honey. Stir to combine and melt the butter (don't worry if it doesn't melt fully). Once the milk mixture has cooled to a maximum of 35°C (95°F), add to the dry ingredients along with the egg.

Knead on a lightly oiled work surface or on a medium speed in a mixer for around 8–10 minutes until the dough is smooth and elastic. Drain the sultanas well, ensuring no excess water remains, and combine them with the mixed peel. Add to the dough and knead for a further 5–10 minutes.

Transfer the dough to a lightly oiled bowl, cover and leave to prove somewhere warm for about 2 hours, or until doubled in size.

Grease a 20cm (8in) square baking tin and line with baking parchment. Once the dough has proved, remove from the bowl and divide it into nine evenly sized balls (around 60g/2½oz each).

On a lightly floured surface, roll each piece of dough into a smooth ball. Arrange the dough balls evenly in the baking tin. Cover with a damp tea towel or pop in a large plastic bag and leave to prove for a further 1–1½ hours, or until almost doubled in size and 'poofy'.

While the buns prove, prepare the glaze. Combine the sugar, water and honey in a small saucepan and place over a low heat, stirring until the sugar dissolves. Bring to the boil and simmer for 1 minute before removing from the heat. Add the whole spices and leave to infuse.

Preheat the oven to 200°C/180°C fan/400°F/Gas 6.

Prepare the piping paste mixture by combining the flour and sugar in a small bowl, then gradually adding the water (you may not need it all) until it forms a smooth, pipeable paste. Transfer to a piping bag fitted with a small round nozzle.

Notes

Soaking the sultanas prevents them from burning when the hot cross buns bake.

'Scalding' the milk for the dough denatures the proteins that can inhibit the action of yeast, thus ensuring a better rise to your dough.

To veganize this dough, use dairy-free alternatives for the butter and milk, remove the egg and sub in 30ml (1¼fl oz) extra dairy-free milk. Use agave nectar in place of the honey or simply an equivalent weight in caster sugar. Instead of an egg wash, use dairy-free milk.

Change up the flavours: add 50g (2oz) dark chocolate chips and the zest of an orange for a chocolate orange vibe, or replace some of the fruit with a handful of dried cranberries and pair with 50g (2oz) white chocolate chips (you could also omit the caster sugar if doing this, to avoid it being too sweet).

Once the buns have risen, pipe a heart or spiral on top of each bun and bake in the oven for 18–20 minutes, or until golden on top and baked through (the internal temperature of the bun should read around 90°C/194°F on a digital thermometer).

Remove the buns from the tin using the parchment to ease them out. Transfer to a wire rack and remove the parchment from underneath.

Using a pastry brush, coat the tops of the buns with the glaze and allow to cool for at least 15 minutes before you dive in. Smear with a good wedge of salty butter and fall into a blissful, doughy dream.

Forest Fruit Frangipane Tartlets

Makes
12 tartlets

Hands-on time
25 minutes + 4¾ hours resting time

Cooking time
45 minutes

Shortcrust pastry scares me, because it requires patience (which I don't have), a delicate touch (not my strong point) and relies, to a certain extent, on some careful planning and time management (and I'm generally quite spontaneous with my baking).

However, there is something incredibly rewarding about producing a bake that is the product of multiple stages, various components, some dedicated time and a little precision. Besides my slightly contentious relationship with shortcrust, I've always had a bit of a thing for Bakewell tarts – the soft, fragrant frangipane and sticky jam are what entice me, and a delicate, crisp shortcrust vessel is the perfect contrast to those elements. Here, I've opted for a simple forest fruit jam combined with a wonderfully light almond frangipane spiked with lemon zest.

Almond pastry

200g (7oz) plain flour, plus extra for dusting

80g (3oz) icing sugar

¼ tsp baking powder

100g (3½oz) cold unsalted butter, cubed

50g (2oz) egg (about 1 large egg)

30g (1¼oz) ground almonds

Forest fruit jam

300g (11oz) fresh or frozen and thawed forest fruits (my favourites are blackberries, blackcurrants, cherries and blueberries)

100g (3½oz) caster sugar

Squeeze of lemon juice

Frangipane

1 tbsp self-raising flour, sifted

110g (3¾oz) ground almonds

110g (3¾oz) unsalted butter, softened

110g (3¾oz) caster sugar

2 large eggs, lightly beaten

½ tsp almond extract

Zest of ½ lemon

Decoration

20g (¾oz) flaked almonds

Icing sugar, for dusting

First, prepare the pastry. Combine the flour, icing sugar and baking powder in a food processor and pulse a few times to combine. Add the butter and pulse until the mixture resembles fine breadcrumbs. Next, add the egg and pulse until just clumping together. Finally, tip in the ground almonds and pulse just until the mixture comes together.

Tip out the pastry onto a large square of cling film, and use the cling film to gently flatten it into a disc. Chill for at least 4 hours.

Meanwhile, prepare the jam. Put the fruit, sugar and lemon juice in a large saucepan over a medium heat and bring to the boil. Simmer for 10–15 minutes, or until the mixture thickens, breaking down the fruits a bit with the back of a spoon about halfway through. Once thickened, remove from the heat and transfer to a bowl to cool completely.

Once the dough has rested, roll it out on a lightly dusted work surface to around 3mm (⅛in) thick. Use a 10cm (4in) pastry cutter to stamp out 12 rounds. Carefully ease the pastry circles into the holes of a muffin pan, gently pressing down – there will be a very slight overhang of pastry, which will be trimmed later. Refrigerate for at least 30 minutes.

Meanwhile, preheat the oven to 180°C/160°C fan/350°F/Gas 4. Place a large baking tray in the oven to heat up.

Prepare the frangipane. Combine the flour and ground almonds in a bowl and gently mix to combine. In a separate bowl, beat together the butter and sugar until light and fluffy. Add the eggs a little at a time, beating well between each addition (don't worry if the mixture starts to curdle a little). Add the almond extract and lemon juice and beat to combine. Finally, add the ground almond mixture and gently fold through until just incorporated. Cover until ready to use.

Once the pastry cases have rested, remove them from the fridge. Trim off any excess pastry, spoon a heaped teaspoon of the cooled jam over the base of each tart case, then freeze the cases for 10 minutes (this will prevent the jam from splurging over the top of your frangipane).

Divide the frangipane mixture equally among the pastry cases and bake on the preheated tray for 12 minutes. Remove from the oven, scatter over the flaked almonds and bake for a further 13 minutes, or until risen, golden and a skewer inserted into the frangipane comes out clean. Once baked, remove the tarts from the oven and allow to cool for 10 minutes in the pan. Remove from the pan and transfer to a wire rack before dusting with sifted icing sugar. Serve warm or cooled.

Notes

I have chosen forest fruits for my jam, but you could opt for a more traditional raspberry or cherry flavouring following the same method if you prefer.

At Christmas, I use this as the basis for my mince pies, spreading mincemeat in the base of the pastry cases and topping with the frangipane as above.

You can use different nuts in the frangipane; ground hazelnuts and pistachios work wonderfully with alternative fruit pairings of your choice.

Spiced Sesame and Honey Buns

Makes
9 buns

Hands-on time
30 minutes + 3 hours proving time

Cooking time
20 minutes

If you ever take me out for coffee and 'cake', I will more than likely go rogue and opt for a sweet doughy bread product – I just find them irresistible. These buns are just that: sweet, sticky, doughy, nutty, buttery and an excellent accompaniment to good coffee. They're reminiscent of the classic Scandinavian cinnamon buns, but with a little Middle Eastern flair, filled with rich, nutty tahini and paired with honey to offset the tahini's slight bitterness, as well as cinnamon and cardamom for a touch of warmth. They're a wonderful, relaxing weekend bake... stress-free to prepare and perfect enjoyed curled up with a good book and a cuppa mid-afternoon.

300g (11oz) strong white bread flour, plus extra for dusting

40g (1½oz) caster sugar

5g (1 tsp) sea salt

7g (¼oz) sachet of fast-action dried yeast

150ml (5fl oz) whole milk, lukewarm

1 tbsp extra virgin olive oil

50g (2oz) egg (about 1 large egg)

20g (¾oz) soft unsalted butter, cubed

Filling

1 tbsp light tahini

30g (1¼oz) unsalted butter

50g (2oz) soft light brown sugar

½ tsp ground cardamom

1½ tsp ground cinnamon

3 tbsp sesame seeds, lightly toasted

Glaze

1 tbsp honey

1 tbsp water

Combine the flour and caster sugar in a bowl. Add the salt to one side of the bowl and the yeast to the other. Add the milk, olive oil and egg and bring everything together to form a shaggy dough.

Either by hand or in a mixer, knead for 5–10 minutes until smooth. Add the softened butter and knead again until the dough is smooth and elastic. Cover and leave to prove somewhere warm for 1½–2 hours, or until doubled in size.

While the dough proves, prepare the filling. Combine the tahini, butter, sugar, cardamom, cinnamon and half of the sesame seeds in a bowl. Mix well and set aside until ready to use.

Once the dough has proved, grease a 20 x 20cm (8 x 8in) baking tin and line with baking parchment.

Punch down the dough to deflate and transfer it to a lightly floured work surface. Roll out into a 25 x 40cm (10 x 16in) rectangle. Spread the filling over the dough.

Starting from the longest edge, tightly roll the dough up into a log. Trim the untidy ends, then slice into nine even chunks, about 4cm (1½in) thick. Dip one spiral face of each dough chunk into the remaining toasted sesame seeds. Evenly arrange the buns, sesame seed side down, in the prepared tin (leave a small gap between each bun to allow them to spread). Cover and set aside to prove somewhere warm for a further 45–60 minutes.

Preheat the oven to 200°C/180°C fan/400°F/Gas 6.

Once proved, bake the buns in the oven for 18–20 minutes, or until golden brown and baked through.

Prepare the glaze by combining the honey and water in a small bowl. Once baked, remove the buns from the oven and lightly brush the tops with the honey glaze, then carefully remove from the tin and transfer to a wire rack to cool.

Chocolate Ganache Mousse with a Coffee Cream and Cookie Crumb

Serves
8

Hands-on time
40 minutes + 3 hours
chilling time

Cooking time
15 minutes

Some bakes are about nostalgia, slowing down, being mindful and switching off, whereas others are about speed, releasing pent-up emotion or soothing a dark mood. This chocolate mousse covers all bases – it takes a little patience and finesse (please don't be put off by the apparent technicality of it) but it's fairly quick to prepare; it's elegant and sophisticated while maintaining an element of childhood charm; it can soothe a frazzled mind on a Friday evening just as well as it can impress friends and family at a dinner party.

175g (6oz) good-quality 55–75% dark chocolate

65ml (2½fl oz) whipping cream

58g (2¼oz) egg yolks (from about 3 large eggs; reserve the whites for meringues)

50g (2oz) egg (about 1 large egg)

70g (2¾oz) caster sugar

275ml (9¾fl oz) double cream

Cookie crumb

25g (1oz) dark chocolate

15g (½oz) unsalted butter, melted

20g (¾oz) cocoa powder

30g (1¼oz) golden caster sugar

15g (½oz) plain flour

Pinch of sea salt

Coffee cream

250ml (8fl oz) double cream

20g (¾oz) icing sugar, sifted

3 tsp instant coffee, dissolved in 1 tsp water

This method of making a mousse is referred to as the *pâte à bombe* method – it ensures that the eggs are cooked and therefore entirely safe to eat but also generates a stable mousse that can be used for cakes as well as a dessert like this.

Put the chocolate into a large heatproof bowl. Heat the whipping cream in a small saucepan to almost boiling and pour over the chocolate, then leave for 5 minutes before gently stirring – if some chocolate remains unmelted, place the bowl over a pan of very gently simmering water and heat until a smooth, glossy ganache forms. Set aside to cool to 40–45°C (104–113°F).

Meanwhile, put the egg yolks and egg into the bowl of a stand mixer and whisk briefly before adding the caster sugar. Remove the bowl and place it over a pan of gently simmering water. Stir and heat to 60°C (140°F). Return the bowl to the mixer and whisk on medium-high speed for 5–10 minutes until the bowl of the mixer is cool to touch, the mixture is almost white and it leaves a trail when you lift out the whisk.

Whisk the double cream just to soft peaks, then cover and refrigerate until ready to use.

Once the chocolate ganache mixture has cooled, fold in the whipped eggs. Mix briefly until just combined. Finally, fold the egg and chocolate mixture into the whipped cream. Divide the mixture between eight small ramekins or cups and refrigerate for 2–3 hours until set.

For the cookie crumb, put the chocolate into a heatproof bowl over a pan of gently simmering water and stir until melted. Remove from the heat and add the butter, cocoa powder, sugar, flour and salt. Mix until a dough forms.

Transfer the dough to a piece of baking parchment, cover with a second piece of parchment and roll out to around 3mm (⅛in) thick. Refrigerate for 10–15 minutes until just firm.

Meanwhile, preheat the oven to180°C/160°C fan/350°F/Gas 4. Remove the cookie crumb dough from fridge, peel away the top layer of parchment, transfer to a baking tray and bake for 15 minutes, or until firm and crisp. Remove from the oven and set aside to cool.

Finally, prepare the coffee cream. Combine the cream, sifted icing sugar and coffee mixture in a bowl and whisk to soft peaks. When ready to serve, dollop the coffee cream on top of the set mousse and sprinkle over some of the cookie crumb.

Mocha Madeleines

Wake up early, whip up a batch of coffee madeleine batter, give it a little rest; meanwhile, you do the same – nip back to bed and have a snooze. Around mid-morning, just when you're starting to feel peckish, get your bake on, stare through your oven door and admire your little cakes as they rise. Once baked and displaying their characteristic hump, remove from the oven, allow to cool, dunk in a little chocolate ganache and serve with, you guessed it, a strong coffee. You will, quite literally, be on cloud nine as you sink your teeth into these wonderfully light little sponges.

Makes
16 madeleines

Hands-on time
20 minutes + 1½ hours resting time

Cooking time
12 minutes

10ml (2 tsp) whole milk

2 tsp espresso powder

100g (3½oz) plain flour, plus extra for dusting

½ tsp baking powder

2 large eggs

80g (3oz) caster sugar

15g (½oz) soft light brown sugar

Pinch of sea salt

15g (½oz) runny honey

100g (3½oz) unsalted butter, melted, plus extra for greasing

Cacao nibs, for sprinkling (optional)

Coffee liqueur ganache

55g (2¼oz) dark chocolate, finely chopped (or chocolate chips)

60ml (2½fl oz) double cream

1½ tsp coffee liqueur (such as Kahlua or Tia Maria)

Combine the milk and espresso powder in a small jug and very gently heat, either on the hob or for 10 seconds in the microwave. Sift the flour and baking powder into a bowl and set aside.

In a large bowl, combine the eggs and sugars and whisk with an electric hand mixer until light and frothy. Add the salt, honey and espresso/milk mixture and whisk again until just incorporated. Next, add the sifted flour and baking powder in two stages, folding in with a spatula. Finally, add the melted butter and fold once more to incorporate. Cover the batter and refrigerate for a minimum of 1½ hours, or overnight.

Meanwhile, grease a 12-hole madeleine tray with melted butter and dust lightly with flour. Place the tray in the fridge until ready to use. Preheat the oven to 200°C/180°C fan/400°F/Gas 6.

When the batter has rested, distribute it evenly among the madeleine holes, filling to around three-quarters full. Don't overfill the madeleine holes. Instead, reserve any extra batter to bake off later, following the same process of greasing, flouring, and chilling the tray – or use a second tray if you have one.

Bake in the oven for 2 minutes before dropping the oven temperature to 180°C/160°C fan/350°F/Gas 4 and continuing to bake for a further 9–10 minutes, or until golden brown and the characteristic hump has formed. Leave to cool in the tin for a couple of minutes before transferring to a wire rack to cool a little.

Prepare the ganache. Put the chocolate into a heatproof bowl and set aside. Pour the cream and coffee liqueur into a small saucepan over a medium heat and heat until almost boiling, then remove from the heat and pour over the chocolate. Allow to stand for 5 minutes before gently stirring to form a smooth ganache (if a few chocolate chips don't melt properly, microwave for 10 seconds and stir again, or place over a pan of barely simmering water until a glossy mixture forms). Allow to cool and thicken up for about 15 minutes.

Once cooled, dunk a madeleine into the chocolate, just enough to cover the curved end around a one-quarter of the way up, then place on a plate or wire rack and repeat with the remaining madeleines. Sprinkle with cacao nibs if desired.

Note

This flavour combination never fails, but my other favorite is citrus – add the grated zest of a lemon, lime or half an orange in place of the coffee, and swap the milk for citrus juice.

'Mince Pie' Eccles Cakes

Serves
8–10

Hands-on time
45 minutes

Cooking time
25 minutes + 2 hours
chilling time

I've never been a massive Christmas fan, but I do love the merriment that accompanies the festive season. For me, a fragile little buttery tart filled with sticky dried fruit epitomizes the very essence of Christmas: rich, luxurious, scented, spiced and often a little boozy. Despite my enjoyment of a mince pie, they can sometimes be a bit disappointing – dry, sparsely filled, lacking in flavour, too sweet or sometimes sour. So, I set out on a mission to create an upgrade, fusing it with another classic, the Eccles cake. Firstly, I opted for a rich puff pastry flavoured with some nutty wholemeal flour. This encases a wonderfully spiced fruit and nut filling bound with some butter to keep it moist. Finally, these little pastries are coated with a sprinkle of demerara sugar for added crunch. Best served slightly warm with a drizzle of cream or brandy butter, they're a bit of alright, I think!

Rough puff pastry

185g (6½oz) plain flour,
plus extra for dusting

40g (1½oz) wholemeal
flour

½ tsp sea salt

165g (5¾oz) cold unsalted
butter, cubed

90ml (3¼fl oz) ice-cold
water

1 tsp white wine vinegar

Filling

50g (2oz) raisins

50g (2oz) sultanas

25g (1oz) dried cranberries

35g (1¼oz) mixed peel

10g (¼oz) crystallized
stem ginger

20g (¾oz) flaked almonds

Zest of ½ large orange

1 tsp ground cinnamon

1 tsp mixed spice

¼ tsp ground nutmeg

Pinch of cloves

45g (1¾oz) demerara sugar

45g (1¾oz) unsalted
butter, melted

Topping

1 small egg, beaten

Demerara sugar, to sprinkle

Combine the flours and salt in a mixing bowl. Add the butter and toss around in the flour, rubbing and pressing the butter into the flour using your fingertips until the mixture contains irregularly sized pieces of butter.

Slowly trickle in the water and white wine vinegar, stirring with a knife. Give it a very gentle knead in the bowl and as soon as the mixture starts to hold together, tip it out onto a lightly floured work surface. Use your hands to gather the dough together into a rough but uniform dough, shape it into a rectangle and wrap in cling film. Chill for 30 minutes.

Remove the dough from the fridge and roll it into a 40 x 15cm (16 x 6in) rectangle. Starting at one of the shorter edges, fold the top half of the dough into the centre, then fold the bottom half into the centre as well, and finally fold the two halves over one another. This is a double fold. Rotate the dough a quarter turn and repeat, rolling it back out and folding as before. Wrap in cling film and chill for a further 30 minutes.

After this time, take the dough back out and lay it on the work surface with the open seams facing towards you, then roll the dough out for its final double fold and refrigerate again for at least 1 hour.

Meanwhile, prepare the filling. Combine everything in a large bowl and mix well to combine. Set aside to cool, then refrigerate to firm up a little.

Preheat the oven to 200°C/180°C fan/400°F/Gas 6. Line a baking tray with baking parchment.

Remove the chilled dough from the fridge and roll out on a lightly floured surface to 3–4mm (around ⅛in) thick – I aim for a 35cm (14in) square. Use 7cm (2¾in) and 8cm (3 ¼in) round cutters to stamp out an equal number of circles of each size.

Dollop a heaped tablespoon of filling into the centre of each of the smaller rounds (you may not need it all). Wet the outside of the dough with cold water and place a larger round of pastry on top, pressing around the edges to seal.

Place on the prepared baking tray and cut three slits in the the top of each pie. Brush with the beaten egg and sprinkle with demerara sugar.

Bake in the oven for 20–25 minutes, or until puffed up and golden brown. Serve warm or cool with cream or brandy butter.

Notes

The vinegar in the pastry helps to prevent discolouration of the dough and makes rolling out a little easier.

Making pastry is a faff, I know. It's absolutely worth it, but if you're in a hurry, by all means use shop-bought puff pastry – it will more than suffice.

If you do make your pastry, for goodness' sake do not waste your scraps! Palmiers are my favourite thing to make with pastry scraps – you can dust them with cinnamon sugar or sprinkle with grated Parmesan for a savoury option.

Mini Spiced Pavlovas with Baked Plums

Pavlova is fairly established as a summer dessert; meringue, piled with cream and scattered with berries or tropical fruits, shrieks of barbecue season and warm evenings enjoyed with friends and family.

However, I firmly believe it's too good not to be enjoyed year-round, I've therefore come up with an autumn/winter spin on the summery classic. A lightly spiced meringue – the perfect balance between 'mallowy' and chewy – topped with a generous helping of crème fraîche and balanced with sticky spiced baked plums. I've also reduced the terror and jeopardy of a large pavlova by making individual little meringues that can be kept in an airtight container and hauled out as an emergency dessert on demand.

This pudding, warming in flavour yet delicate on the palate, is the perfect antidote to a rich main course – it's hard not to love!

Serves
6

Hands-on time
40 minutes + 4 hours or overnight cooling time

Cooking time
2¾ hours

Meringue

80g (3oz) egg whites (from about 2 large eggs)
140g (4¾oz) caster sugar
¼ tsp ground cinnamon
⅛ tsp ground nutmeg
Pinch of ground cloves
1 tsp cornflour
1 tsp white wine vinegar
Crème fraîche, to serve

Baked plums

6 medium purple plums (about 400g/14oz total), stoned and quartered
110ml (3¾fl oz) freshly squeezed orange juice
Zest of ½ large orange
15g (½oz) golden caster sugar
¼ tsp ground cinnamon
1 star anise
1 cinnamon stick
10g (¼oz) crystallized stem ginger, chopped

Notes

To preserve egg yolks for use in curds or mousses, cover with a little cold water and store in an airtight container in the fridge. Use within 2–4 days and drain the water when you come to use them.

I like to prepare the plums the day before if I have time, as it intensifies their flavour.

Preheat the oven to 130°C/110°C fan/250°F/Gas ½. Line a baking tray with baking parchment.

Place the egg whites into the bowl of a clean, degreased stand mixer and whisk on medium-high speed until medium peaks (resembling cappuccino foam) form. Lower the speed and slowly add the sugar, 1 teaspoon at a time – this should take around 3 minutes. Once all the sugar has been added, continue to whisk on medium-low speed for 15 minutes, or until it is thick, shiny, forms stiff peaks and the sugar has fully dissolved.

Add the spices and continue to mix on low speed, before adding the cornflour and vinegar. Whisk for a final 30 seconds, or until well combined.

Dollop six mounds of the mixture onto the baking tray and bake for 2 hours, or until the meringue pulls away from the parchment. Leave to cool in the oven, with the door propped open, for 4 hours, or overnight.

Meanwhile, prepare the plums. Preheat the oven to 200°C/180°C fan/400°F/Gas 6. Put the plums in a roasting dish. Combine the orange juice and zest, sugar and ground cinnamon in a small bowl. Pour over the plums, coating them evenly. Add the star anise, cinnamon stick and chopped crystallized ginger and bake in the oven for 10 minutes.

Remove the plums from the oven and baste them with the juices from the dish. Cover with foil and return to the oven to cook for 10–30 minutes until softened but still holding their shape. Remove from the oven and set aside, covered, to cool and macerate in the syrup.

To serve, top each meringue with a hefty dollop of crème fraîche before adding a couple of plum quarters and their juices.

Tiramisu Cake

I adore Italy and everything about it: the weather, the food (and drink), the coffee, the way of life, the people... I could go on! It's probably no surprise, then, that I'm a big fan of tiramisu. It's just everything I could ask for: coffee, mascarpone, cake, a touch of booze, chocolate – the dream! I wouldn't dare try to replicate the classic as I'm never going to live up to those served in Italian trattorias, but I was keen to pay homage to my love for the country (and this dessert) in some capacity, so I conjured up a tiramisu cake. Layers of delicately infused tender coffee sponge, drenched in a Marsala coffee syrup, interspersed with a mascarpone frosting and chocolate ganache, coated with more frosting and decorated with some chocolate curls and a dusting of cocoa powder. It may not be the real deal, but it's a pretty decent alternative, and, to me, it is the essence of slowing down to find pleasure in simple, soothing things.

Serves
10

Hands-on time
1¼ hours

Cooking time
25 minutes

1 tbsp whole milk

1 tbsp espresso powder

60g (2½oz) sour cream

1 tsp vanilla extract

180g (6¼oz) unsalted butter, softened

110g (3¾oz) caster sugar

70g (2¾oz) soft light brown sugar

3 large eggs

180g (6¼oz) plain flour

2¼ tsp baking powder

Pinch of sea salt

Marsala coffee syrup

75g (2¾oz) caster sugar

75ml (2¾fl oz) very strong hot coffee (or 1½ tbsp espresso powder mixed with 5 tbsp water)

45ml (1¾fl oz) Marsala (or dark rum)

Chocolate ganache

75g (2¾oz) 54% dark chocolate

75ml (2¾fl oz) double cream

Mascarpone frosting

115g (3¾oz) unsalted butter, softened

250g (9oz) icing sugar, sifted

200g (7oz) cream cheese, at room temperature

100g (3½oz) mascarpone, at room temperature

To decorate

50g (2oz) white chocolate

1 tbsp cocoa powder

A small handful of coffee beans

20g (¾oz) chocolate curls or grated milk chocolate

Prepare the Marsala coffee syrup first. Heat the sugar and coffee in a small saucepan over a medium heat until the sugar has dissolved. Turn up the heat and bring to the boil, then simmer for 5 minutes before stirring in the Marsala. Set aside to cool.

Next make the cake. Preheat the oven to 180°C/160°C fan/350°F/Gas 4. Grease three 15cm (6in) cake tins and line with baking parchment.

Slightly warm the milk and combine with the espresso powder in a small bowl. Stir until dissolved, then add the sour cream and vanilla extract and stir well to combine. Set aside.

Combine the butter and sugars in the bowl of a stand mixer or a large bowl and beat on a medium speed for about 5 minutes until light, fluffy and increased in volume. Add the eggs one at a time, beating thoroughly between each addition.

Sift together the flour, baking powder and salt in a bowl, then gently fold it into the wet ingredients, alternating with the sour cream mixture, until mixed.

Divide the cake batter evenly between the prepared tins and bake in the oven for 20–25 minutes, or until risen, golden and a skewer inserted into the cake comes out clean. Once baked, allow the cakes to cool in their tins for 5 minutes before turning out onto a wire rack to cool completely.

While the cakes cool, prepare the chocolate ganache. Put the chocolate into a heatproof bowl. Heat the cream in a small saucepan until just boiling, then pour it over the chocolate. Leave to stand before mixing to make a smooth ganache, then leave to set to a spreadable consistency.

For the mascarpone frosting, measure the butter into a saucepan and heat until just melted – not piping hot. Remove from the heat and set aside while you prepare the remaining ingredients. Sift the icing sugar into a large bowl, add the cream cheese and mascarpone and gently beat with an electric hand mixer until just smooth. With the mixer still on a low speed, gradually pour the melted butter into the mascarpone mixture until completely combined and smooth. If the butter was a little warm, the consistency may be a little loose; chill in the fridge for 20 minutes or so or until it's a little firmer if needed.

For the white chocolate decorations, melt the white chocolate in a heatproof bowl placed over a pan of gently simmering water. Once melted and smooth, pour onto a lined baking tray and spread to a thickness of about 3mm (⅛in). Refrigerate to set firm.

Once set, use three different sized round cookie cutters, gently heated, to stamp out round discs. Put back into the fridge once shaped, until ready to use.

To assemble, halve each of the cakes horizontally. Brush the open crumb face of each cake round liberally with the marsala coffee syrup, until it is all used up.

Place one cake disc on a cake board, spread over a thin layer of frosting, then add a second cake layer. This time spread over a thin layer of the ganache. Repeat, alternating layers of frosting and ganache, before adding the final sponge.

Once the cake is assembled, spread more frosting around the outside of the cake and over the top to create a crumb coat. Transfer to the fridge to set a little before applying a second neat, thin coat of frosting.

To decorate, dust cocoa powder over the top of the cake, then top with a sprinkling of coffee beans, chocolate curls or grated chocolate and the white chocolate discs.

Happy
Place

Research demonstrates that memories involving food are often very vivid. I remember a pudding we were served at school that was so devilish that I'd resort to smuggling out second helpings in my pocket (it was messy), garlic bread from my favourite local Italian restaurant served on a metal stand and dripping with garlic-infused herby butter, rice crispy treats purchased from the school tuck shop for 20p and, most notably, a pizza bianca I picked up from a little bakery in Rome (Forno Campo de' Fiori). The flavour was magical: creamy, authentic Italian cheese laced with extra virgin olive oil and garnished with a sprinkling of fresh rocket – so simple yet truly sublime. (Incidentally, if you go to Rome, please put this on your list of places to visit!)

Food memories are strong because they involve all five senses, and food nostalgia is thought to be so vivid due to the biological need for nourishment – an ability to retain information regarding the source of food when it was scarce was crucial for survival. Not only that, but the area of the brain involved in memory works closely with regions of the brain involved in emotion regulation and smell, so a food memory is often triggered by the subtlest of aromas – think baking bread – and accompanied by strong emotions. Fascinating!

Similarly, 'comfort foods' are reported to provide genuine psychological benefits due to the possible release of the neurotransmitter dopamine into the body, which confers rewards such as pleasure and stress relief. These feelings are often accompanied by deep memories that can include caring and love – ultimately boosting our moods in times of need.

Nothing makes me happier than stepping into the kitchen to recreate something I have a fond memory of, as it takes me back to the moment I first enjoyed it. Not only do I experience all the meditative benefits of baking, the delectable outcome and the boost in confidence, but I also reignite joyful moments from the past, remembering loved ones, old friends and beautiful places. Sharing the bake with others doubles the immediate happiness and creates a new memory, which is saved for future foodie pleasure.

I'm aware that what constitutes a nostalgic bake or comfort food is very personal, so what you will find in the following pages are a few of my favourites. I hope some of them can bring out some happy memories for you too. Consider this a chance to think back to some of your own fondest foodie memories: sticky toffee pudding in a pub after a long winter walk, arctic roll on a warm summer's day in the garden, fig rolls inhaled after a school hockey match, or sticky iced fingers – the possibilities are endless and with a little recipe research, you can recreate wonderful joyful moments.

Pizza Dough Balls with Garlic Browned Butter

When refining the recipes for this book, I included my friends and family a lot… in fact, they have contributed to this almost as much as I have. They have been subjected to plenty of taste tests and me giving them a hard time if they are not enthusiastic enough or don't provide sufficient feedback! This one is for Harriet and Simon: they both requested pizza dough balls with garlic butter and frankly, I don't blame them. I remember visiting Italian restaurants as a kid and eating so much garlic bread that my main course was totally sidelined.

Makes
10 balls

Hands-on time
25 minutes

Cooking time
25 minutes + 3 hours proving time

Add the malt extract to the water and stir to dissolve. Put the flour, salt and yeast into a bowl, keeping the salt and yeast on separate sides of the bowl. Pour the water and malt mixture into the bowl and use your hand or a spoon to bring the dough together into a shaggy mass. Leave to rest for 20 minutes.

Once rested, knead for 10–15 minutes, or until very elastic and smooth. Transfer to a lightly oiled bowl, cover and leave to prove somewhere warm for around 2 hours, or until doubled in size.

Heaped ½ tsp malt extract

140ml (4¾fl oz) tepid water

200g (7oz) strong white bread flour

Scant 1 tsp sea salt

1 tsp fast-action dried yeast

Meanwhile, prepare the garlic butter. Heat the olive oil in a small saucepan over a medium heat. Add the grated garlic and cook for 1 minute, stirring to ensure it doesn't catch. Transfer to a plate to cool.

Garlic and parsley butter

½ tsp olive oil

½ garlic clove, grated

50g (2oz) unsalted butter

1 tbsp finely chopped parsley

⅛ tsp flaky sea salt

While the garlic cools, brown the butter. Melt the butter in a small saucepan over a medium heat, stirring periodically. Once the butter has melted, it will splatter and spit before a foam forms on top.

Once the foam starts to appear, look for signs of browning – there should be a nutty, toasted aroma and the milk solids will turn a golden brown at the bottom of the pan. Be careful not to keep it on the heat too long at this point or it will go too far and burn. Remove from the heat, transfer to a bowl and leave to cool before refrigerating to solidify.

Once solidified, beat together with the fried garlic, chopped parsley and flaky sea salt. Transfer to a small bowl and leave at room temperature until the dough balls are ready.

Line two baking trays with baking parchment. Knock the dough back and shape into ten dough balls of about 30g (1¼oz). Transfer the dough balls to the lined baking trays, spaced well apart. Cover and leave to prove again for 45–60 minutes.

Preheat the oven to 240°C/220°C fan/475°F/Gas 9 and place a baking stone (or baking tray) inside to heat up for at least 30 minutes. Once the dough balls are ready, carefully transfer half of them to the baking stone, using the parchment to transfer them across. Bake for 8–10 minutes, or until puffed up and golden.

Once baked, remove from the oven and leave to cool for 5–10 minutes while you bake the second batch. Serve with the garlic and parsley butter, either melted and gently brushed over the dough balls, or served on the side for dipping.

Notes

These will still be delicious even if you don't brown the butter; it just adds another layer of flavour.

You can adapt these dough balls to suit any occasion; all sorts of herbs work fabulously when stirred through butter, as do sun-dried tomatoes and grated Parmesan with basil for a pizza vibe or chilli, coriander and lime for a more Asian flavour.

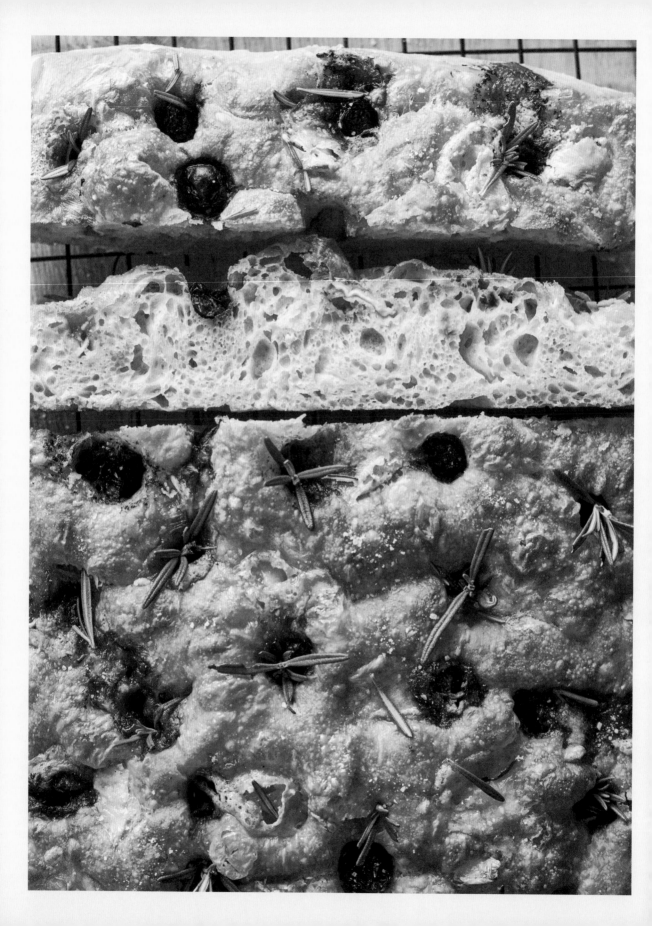

Lazy Goat's Cheese, Grape and Rosemary Focaccia

I seem to have a reputation among my baking friends (Rosie in particular) for my love of bread and oil. Chuck some cheese in there, essentially making a pizza bread, and I'm a happy girl. Focaccia encapsulates this love affair, and what makes it even better is its simplicity, in both concept and construction. Throw a handful of quality ingredients together the night before you plan to bake, no kneading required, plop it into a tin, give it a second rise, prod it with your fingers and add your favourite toppings, bake and devour. It's versatile, lasts well and (of course) tastes great. What's not to love?

I've opted for sweet and salty flavours here, with the cheese and grape combination that was popular in the noughties – it seemed like a real revelation at the time. Coupled with a little rosemary, it is a wonderful adornment to the traditional oily focaccia dough.

~~~~~~~~~~~~~~~~~

Serves
12

Hands-on time
10–15 minutes
+ 15 hours proving time

Cooking time
25–30 minutes

500g (1lb 2oz) strong white bread flour

440ml (14¾fl oz) lukewarm water

10g (2 tsp) sea salt

7g (¼oz) sachet of fast-action dried yeast

3 tsp, plus 2 tbsp olive oil, plus extra for greasing

Topping

100g (3½oz) grapes

100g (3½oz) firm goat's cheese (I like Kidderton Ash), cut into cubes

3 rosemary sprigs, leaves picked

Extra virgin olive oil, for drizzling

Balsamic vinegar, to serve

Flaky sea salt

Combine the flour, water, salt and yeast in a bowl and mix with a wooden spoon or spatula, ensuring the ingredients are well combined and no lumps of flour remain, then add 2 teaspoons of the oil and mix again with the spatula.

Once homogenous, scrape down the sides of the bowl and drizzle another teaspoon of the olive oil over the top of the dough. Cover and transfer to the fridge to prove overnight, or for a minimum of 12 hours.

The following day, lightly grease a 23 x 33cm (9 x 13in) tin and line with baking parchment. Drizzle the 2 tablespoons of olive oil into the lined tin.

Remove the dough from the fridge, punch down to deflate and plop it out into the tin. Using oiled hands, fold the dough in on itself from each of the four sides, then flip over so that the seam is underneath and leave to prove for a further 2–3 hours.

Once the dough has spread out and is bubbly, it is ready. Preheat the oven to 220°C/200°C fan/ 425°F/Gas 7.

Liberally oil your hands and dimple the dough with your fingertips all over. Push in the grapes, cheese cubes and the rosemary leaves, distributing evenly over the surface.

Drizzle over some olive oil and sprinkle with a pinch of flaky sea salt. Bake in the oven for 25–30 minutes, or until the underside is golden and crisp.

Once baked, remove from the oven and transfer to a cooling rack to cool. Serve with more oil, sea salt and a drizzle of balsamic vinegar, or split and use as bread for the most epic sandwiches.

Notes

Here are a few other great flavour combos you could try:

- **Greek flavours:** halloumi or feta, paired with olive, tomato and herbs such as parsley, coriander, basil and/or oregano, finished with a sprinkling of sesame or nigella seeds.

- **Middle Eastern-style:** sprinkle with za'atar.

- **Traditional Italian:** top with olive and tomato – this simple combination just works.

- **Red onion and rosemary with pesto ricotta:** finely slice a red onion and pair with the rosemary and salt before baking. Whip up a couple of large spoonfuls of ricotta, stir through a tablespoon of pesto and serve alongside your focaccia – yum!

Lemon Rosemary Crackers

We have already established that I have my quirks, but here is another one: I really am obsessed with savoury crackers. I'd rather have an oatcake than a chocolate digestive or a seeded flatbread over a custard cream any day! I have fond memories of a childhood trip to Hong Kong with Mum, which included some serious jetlag and midnight feasts of crackers in bed, with crumbs for company. Over time the love affair has grown – crackers and cheese, the ultimate meal; if I'm feeling a bit sick, hand me a cracker; for dinner party dips, only crackers will suffice.

These lemon and rosemary crackers really are the pinnacle of crackers. Yes, the process is somewhat elaborate, but I promise you they are worth it – buttery, crisp, flaky, salty and aromatic, they just hit the spot. Controversial statement here, but I think they're better than crisps.

∿∿∿∿∿∿∿∿∿∿∿∿∿∿∿∿∿∿∿

Makes
about 50 crackers

Hands-on time
35 minutes + about 7 hours fermenting and resting time

Cooking time
20–25 minutes per batch

Pre-ferment

40g (1½oz) wholemeal bread flour

60g (2½oz) strong white bread flour

⅛ tsp fast-action dried yeast

100ml (3½fl oz) water

Dough

100g (3½oz) plain flour, plus extra for dusting

1 tbsp sesame seeds

1 tsp dried rosemary

Zest of ½ lemon

½ tsp sea salt

50g (2oz) unsalted butter, softened

Topping

2 tbsp olive oil

½ tsp dried rosemary (optional)

Flaky sea salt

To serve

Hummus, cheese or other dips and toppings of your choice

Note

If you have a sourdough starter kicking around and are left with some pesky discard that needs using up, use that in place of the pre-ferment – it yields biscuits that are just as good and have a subtle, sour tang.

First prepare the pre-ferment. In a medium-sized bowl, combine the flours, yeast and water and stir with a wooden spoon to form a sticky mixture. Cover and leave to ferment in a warm place for about 4–5 hours, or until at least doubled in volume – it should be a bit bubbly. You could also leave it to rise overnight if preferred.

Once risen, prepare the cracker dough. Combine the plain flour, sesame seeds, rosemary, lemon zest and salt in a large mixing bowl and mix well. Add the cold butter and rub into the dry ingredients until the mixture resembles coarse breadcrumbs.

Add the pre-ferment and use a knife to cut it into the dry ingredients before using your hand to gently bring the mixture together to form a dough – you don't want to overwork the mixture but you can very delicately knead the mixture to bring it together.

Once combined, cover in cling film and rest in the fridge for at least 2 hours – again, you can leave overnight if that fits your schedule better.

Once the dough has rested, preheat the oven to 170°C/150°C fan/325°F/Gas 3 and line two large baking trays with parchment.

Remove the dough from the fridge, split in half and wrap one piece back in the cling film and return to the fridge. With the remaining piece, lightly flour the work surface and use a rolling pin to roll out as thin as you can. Keep dusting the work surface and rolling pin with flour where necessary – I usually end up with a roughly 30 x40cm (12 x 16in) rectangle.

Once rolled out, carefully roll the dough up and around the rolling pin and gently transfer to one of the lined trays. Pour half of the olive oil into a small ramekin and use a pastry brush to gently brush over the dough. Sprinkle with a few sea salt crystals and some dried rosemary, if using.

Use a pizza slice or sharp knife to cut the dough into about 25 pieces in any fashion you like – I used to go for a uniform shape but I'm terrible at precision, so I tend to veer towards random shapes so that it looks deliberately rustic.

Bake in the oven for 20–25 minutes, or until golden. While the first batch bake, prepare the second batch as above, using up the remaining dough. Serve with hummus, cheese or if you're anything like my family, enjoy them alone.

Cherry Crumble Squares

Makes
16 squares

Hands-on time
20 minutes + 1 hour
macerating time

Cooking time
1 hour 10 minutes

This one is a bit of a throwback for me. During my schooldays, my good friend Emily and I were obsessed with one particular lunchtime dessert, with a shortbread base sticky jam filling and coconut crumble topping – we would smuggle out second (sometimes even third) helpings of this wonder slice. It's arguably a pretty basic concept, but it's utterly addictive. Here I've attempted to replicate it, with all the school-day charm, combined with a touch of adult finesse. Take it with you on a picnic or enjoy as an afternoon pick-me-up with a cup of tea, and prepare yourself for a moment or two of unrivalled bliss.

Shortbread base

160g (5½oz) plain flour

¼ tsp fine sea salt

65g (2½oz) golden caster sugar

130g (4½oz) cold unsalted butter, cubed

Crumble topping

40g (1½oz) light brown muscovado sugar

80g (3oz) unsalted butter

100g (3½oz) plain flour

30g (1¼oz) jumbo oats

20g (¾oz) flaked almonds

15g (½oz) desiccated coconut

Pinch of sea salt

Filling

300g (11oz) cherries, pitted

10g (¼oz) golden caster sugar

2 tsp lemon juice

¼–½ tsp almond extract

Pinch of sea salt

10g (¼oz) cornflour

First start the filling. Put the cherries into a bowl and add the sugar, lemon juice, almond extract and salt and leave to macerate for 1 hour.

Preheat the oven to 190°C/170°C fan/375°F/Gas 5. Grease a 20cm (8in) square loose-bottomed cake tin and line with baking parchment.

Prepare the shortbread base. In a large bowl, combine the flour, salt and sugar. Add the cubed butter and rub into the dry ingredients until the mixture resembles fine breadcrumbs (alternatively, you can do this in a food processor or in a stand mixer on the lowest speed using the paddle attachment).

Notes

This recipe is very adaptable:

- Switch up the fruit and use whatever you have to hand, or what's in season.

- Substitute 20g (¾oz) rye, wholegrain or even buckwheat flour into the shortbread base for even more depth of flavour.

- If you don't have any fresh fruit (and have a sweet tooth!), grab a jar of your favourite jam and spread a thin layer over the shortbread base in place of the fruit filling.

- Switch up the nuts in the crumble topping – try coarsely chopped pecans combined with a sprinkle of cinnamon or fennel, for example.

This slice is meant to be served cold, but after a day or two, try popping it back in the oven for 5–10 minutes until warmed through. You'll have yourself a wicked cherry crumble pie dessert! Drizzle with double cream or serve with a scoop of ice cream.

Transfer the mixture to the prepared tin and press down firmly using your fingers or the base of a small glass to form an even layer.

Prick all over with a fork and bake for 15–18 minutes until lightly golden. Once baked, remove from the oven and allow to cool. Reduce the temperature of the oven to 180°C/160°C fan/350°F/Gas 4.

Meanwhile, finish the cherry filling. Transfer the macerated cherry mixture to a saucepan, add the cornflour and stir into the juices. Place over a medium-low heat and cook gently until the mixture just starts to thicken. As soon as the liquid becomes a little thicker and coats the back of a spatula, remove it from the heat and set aside to cool a little.

To make the crumble topping, combine all the ingredients in a bowl and rub everything together to form bigger clumps, rather than breadcrumbs (this can also be done in a stand mixer using the paddle attachment). Refrigerate until needed.

Assemble the squares by spooning the cherry filling over the top of the cooled shortbread base, spreading out evenly. Sprinkle over the crumble topping (it may seem like quite a lot but get it all on there) and bake in the oven for 45–50 minutes, or until golden brown on top and the cherry filling is still slightly bubbling.

Remove from the oven, place on a wire rack and leave to cool in the tin. Cut into squares once fully cooled. Refrigerate leftover squares in an airtight container for up to 5 days.

Baked Raspberry Custard Cream Doughnuts

One of my fondest foodie memories from childhood is Mum picking me up from school on a Friday (her only day off work), greeting me at the school gates with a plump jam doughnut. Because of this I gave them a go myself early on in my baking journey. They weren't a total disaster, but they certainly didn't live up to expectations – overbaked exteriors, raw centres and the jeopardy of searingly hot fat were just a few of my issues. However, worse than any of this was the smell that permeated the house shortly after I started deep-frying – I'm sure people will argue with me here, but for me, it's an awful smell, and to this day I haven't deep-fried a single thing since (shameful, I know, because the results when done right are really worth it).

But, I figured I couldn't go a lifetime without having another go at doughnuts, so I set out on a baked doughnut mission. I was sceptical, as I'm sure you are, too, but after some research, a bit of science wizardry and a little careful tweaking, I swear I have produced something that entirely matches up.

Makes
6 doughnuts

Hands-on time
1 hour + 3½ hours proving time

Cooking time
12 minutes

Doughnuts

90ml (3¼fl oz) whole milk

4g (1 tsp) fast-action dried yeast

40g (1½oz) caster sugar

215g (7½oz) strong white bread flour

50g (2oz) egg (about 1 large egg)

1 heaped tsp runny honey

½ tsp sea salt

Zest of ½ lemon

35g (1¼oz) softened unsalted butter, cubed

Raspberry compote

300g (11oz) fresh or frozen raspberries

80g (3oz) caster sugar

Squeeze of lemon juice

Custard cream

1 large egg yolk

8g (½ tbsp) cornflour

25g (1oz) caster sugar

100ml (3½fl oz) whole milk

½ tsp vanilla bean paste

150ml (5fl oz) double cream

½ tsp vanilla extract

Coating

15g (½oz) butter, melted

50g (2oz) caster sugar

First, pour the milk into a small saucepan, place over a low–medium heat and bring almost to the boil (85°C/185°F on a digital thermometer). Remove from the heat and leave to cool slightly, to around 35°C (95°F). Once the milk has cooled, add the yeast along with 1 teaspoon of the caster sugar. Leave to stand for 10 minutes to bloom.

Meanwhile, combine the flour with the remaining sugar and the egg, honey, salt and lemon zest in the bowl of a stand mixer. Once the yeast has bloomed and the milk mixture is frothy, add it to the bowl. Using the dough hook, knead on a medium speed for 8–10 minutes, then rest the dough in the bowl for 10 minutes.

With the mixer running slowly, add the cubed butter to the dough, allowing each addition to incorporate fully before adding the next (it can get a bit messy but it will come together eventually). Once everything is well combined, knead the dough on a medium speed for a further 5–8 minutes, or until it is smooth and elastic. This can all be done by hand but it will be quite sticky, so be warned. Transfer the dough to a lightly oiled bowl, cover and leave to prove in warm place for around 2 hours, or until increased in volume by half.

Next, prepare the raspberry filling. Combine the raspberries and caster sugar in a medium saucepan, stir to coat the berries in sugar and leave to macerate for a minimum of 15 minutes. Add the lemon juice, stir to combine, then cook over a medium-low heat, stirring occasionally, until the sugar dissolves. Once no sugar crystals remain (check by rubbing a little of the juices between your thumb and forefinger) increase the heat, bring to the boil and simmer, stirring occasionally, for 10 minutes, or until it starts to thicken. Once thickened, remove from the heat and pass through a sieve into a bowl. Set aside to cool.

To make the custard cream, first make a crème pâtissière. Combine the egg yolk, cornflour and sugar in a bowl. Combine the milk and vanilla bean paste in a small saucepan over a low medium heat and bring almost to the boil. Pour the steaming milk over the egg mixture, whisking continually.

Once all the milk has been added, transfer the mixture back to the saucepan and cook over a medium heat, stirring continually, until the mixture thickens. Once thickened, immediately remove from the heat, transfer to a bowl and cover with cling film to prevent a skin forming.

Once the dough has risen, remove it from the bowl and divide it into six 60–70g (2½–2¾oz) chunks. Roll into balls before placing on a lined baking tray. Cover loosely with a damp tea towel or proving bag and leave in a warm place for another 1½ hours until puffy and risen.

Around 30 minutes before the dough has finished proving, preheat the oven to 190°C/170°C fan/375°F/Gas 5. Once ready to bake, uncover the dough and bake for about 12 minutes, or until lightly browned (they should reach around 95°C/203°F in the centre if tested with a digital thermometer).

While the doughnuts are baking, spread the caster sugar for the coating onto a plate. Once baked, remove the doughnuts from the oven, lightly brush with the melted butter and then roll in the sugar, tapping off any excess. Transfer to a wire rack to cool.

While the buns cool, beat the double cream and vanilla extract to medium-stiff peaks. Give the cooled crème pâtissière a quick stir to loosen it, then add to the cream and briefly beat again until combined and holding stiff peaks. Cover and refrigerate until ready to assemble.

To assemble, cut the doughnuts down the middle, leaving a hinge at the bottom. Spread a few teaspoons of the raspberry mixture over one side before loading in some of the custard cream.

Raspberry, Lemon and Pistachio Cake

During my sixth week on Bake Off, I baked a layered pistachio meringue sandwiched with a whipped lemon cream and crushed raspberries... on that occasion, I overbaked the meringue and apparently went a bit overboard with the pistachios – not my finest hour! However, the flavour combination was such a winner that I felt compelled to utilize it again in some other form.

This recipe is super-simple to prepare and bake, incredibly versatile – i.e., you can freestyle with your ingredients – and stays fabulously moist due to the high proportion of nuts. Enjoyed warm or cold, it never fails to deliver.

Serves
12

Hands-on time
15 minutes

Cooking time
1 hour

150g (5oz) whole shelled pistachios

250g (9oz) caster sugar

80g (3oz) plain flour

80g (3oz) ground almonds

1 tsp baking powder

Pinch of sea salt

4 large eggs

200g (7oz) unsalted butter, melted

1 tsp vanilla extract

¼ tsp pistachio extract (or almond extract)

Zest of 3 large lemons

180g (6¼oz) frozen raspberries

30–50g (1¼– 2oz) slivered or chopped pistachios

Greek yoghurt or crème fraîche, to serve

Preheat the oven to 180°C/160°C fan/350°F/Gas 4. Grease a 23cm (9in) round springform cake tin and line the base and sides with baking parchment.

Place the pistachio nuts and half the caster sugar in a food processor and pulse to form to a fine meal – don't over-blend or the mixture will become oily.

Sift the flour into a bowl and add the ground pistachios, along with the remaining caster sugar, the ground almonds, baking powder and salt, and stir gently to combine.

In a separate bowl, lightly whisk the eggs. Add the melted butter, vanilla extract, pistachio (or almond) extract and lemon zest and whisk again until homogenous. Add the wet ingredients to the dry ingredients and whisk to combine.

Pour half of the batter into the prepared cake tin, scatter over about 100g (3½oz) of the raspberries and then top with the remaining batter. Scatter the remaining raspberries over the top of the cake as evenly as possible, followed by the slivered or chopped pistachios.

Bake in the oven for 50–60 minutes, or until a skewer inserted into the centre of the cake comes out clean. Allow to cool in the tin for 30 minutes before turning out onto a wire rack.

This cake can be served warm or cold – it is especially good with a dollop of Greek yoghurt or crème fraîche.

Notes

This cake is a bit of a monster – both in cost and size. It really is worth it, but the following tweaks might make it a little more accessible:

Firstly, you can pare it back and bake the recipe as cupcakes: quarter or halve the recipe to yield four or eight cupcakes respectively, and bake at the same temperature for around 30 minutes, or until a skewer inserted comes out clean.

If you don't have pistachios, you can use almonds – it will be a little different, but the nuts have a similar flavour profile so it still produces an absolute winner.

This recipe also totally works with cherries and blueberries, so don't be afraid to mix up the fruit a bit too.

Apple and Blackberry Sponge Pudding

Serves
4–6

Hands-on time
15 minutes

Cooking time
35–40 minutes

Pudding for me is generally a fruity affair, often as simple as fresh or baked fruit with yoghurt or crème fraîche. However, sometimes a warm sponge pudding with vanilla custard or cream is warranted... I'm talking about cold, dark winter nights when you need some comfort and a little nostalgia. This pudding has a place in my heart because I distinctly remember eating it soon after I had been diagnosed with an eating disorder; I was still underweight and food was scary, but Mum suggested we make this together one evening as she remembered it from her childhood. It was a huge psychological challenge for me at the time, but inevitably was so worth it.

It's not a ground-breaking concept, but it unequivocally delivers both in flavour and satisfaction. Tart juicy apples and blackberries combined with brown sugar and heaps of lemon zest nestle beneath a layer of buttery vanilla sponge. Ladled into bowls still steaming hot, drowned in custard or cream and eaten on the sofa, this pudding is the epitome of foodie joy.

450g (1lb) cooking apples (I use Bramley), peeled, cored and cut into 2.5cm (1in) chunks

35g (1¼oz) demerara sugar

Zest of 1 large or 2 small lemons, plus 1 tbsp juice

100g (3½oz) fresh blackberries (or use frozen, defrosted and thoroughly drained of excess juices)

120g (4oz) unsalted butter

120g (4oz) caster sugar

120g (4oz) egg (about 2 medium eggs)

120g (4oz) self-raising flour, sifted

Pinch of sea salt

1 tsp whole milk

½ tsp vanilla extract

25g (1oz) flaked almonds

Custard, cream, ice cream or crème fraîche, to serve

Preheat the oven to 180°C/160°C fan/350°F/Gas 4. Lightly grease a roughly 17 x 22cm (7 x 9in) ovenproof dish.

Put the apples into a saucepan over a medium heat with the sugar, lemon zest and juice and cook for 5 minutes, or until the sugar has dissolved and the apples are just tender but still holding their shape. Transfer the apple mixture to the prepared dish, levelling it out, and scatter the blackberries evenly over the top. Set aside while you prepare the sponge.

Put the butter and caster sugar in a large bowl and beat until light and fluffy. Add the eggs one at a time, beating well between each addition. Finally, fold through the sifted flour and salt, followed by the milk and vanilla extract.

Spoon the sponge mixture onto the apples and blackberries, level with a palette knife and sprinkle over the flaked almonds,

Bake in the oven for 35–40 minutes, or until golden brown, well risen and a skewer inserted into the sponge comes out clean.

Serve with hot custard, cream, ice cream or crème fraîche for a dose of comfort.

Notes

Dish size is fairly important for this recipe – mine has a capacity of around 1.2 litres (2½ pints) but crucially isn't too deep and narrow. The dimensions listed above are quite common, so if you have something roughly similar, it should be fine.

I love the purity of this recipe. If possible, forage for a handful of blackberries and pick a couple of British apples – it somehow makes this dessert even better. Apples and blackberries are in season in the UK in September and October.

You could also substitute firm pears for the apples and omit the blackberries.

In season, opt for gooseberries, rhubarb, plums or apricots with orange zest instead of lemon.

Zingy Citrus Posset with Blackberry Compote and Shortbread

I remember eating a lemon posset at a friend's house when I was about 16; his mum was a keen foodie, and she was one of the first people to really open my eyes to the diversity of flavours in food. She would make wonderful dinners, including puddings and the occasional sweet bakes for afternoon tea – a real kitchen wizard.

The lemon posset she made blew my mind, it was velvety smooth, sharp yet sweet and, as I later understood, unbelievably simple to throw together. Despite this, it took me a good ten years to give it a go myself – shameful!

This little pot of perfection is perfect if you are entertaining and in need of a stress-free dessert. The zingy posset is served alongside a blackberry compote with complementary sharpness and a coconut and lime shortbread for a little crunch.

Serves
3 (double up for a larger crowd)

Hands-on time
15 minutes + 3½ hours steeping, resting and setting time

Cooking time
30 minutes

220ml (7½oz) double cream

60g (2½oz) caster sugar

Zest and juice of 1 small lemon (30ml/1¼fl oz juice)

Zest and juice of 1 small lime (15ml/½oz juice)

Pinch of sea salt

Coconut and lime shortbread

25g (1oz) caster sugar, plus extra for sprinkling

Zest of ½ large lime

45g (1¾oz) unsalted butter

50g (2oz) plain flour

20g (¾oz) ground almonds

10g (¼oz) desiccated coconut

Pinch of sea salt

Blackberry compote

200g (7oz) frozen blackberries

15g (½oz) caster sugar

Squeeze of lemon juice

1 bay leaf (optional)

Pour the cream into a large saucepan over a low heat and add the sugar, briefly mixing to combine. Once the sugar has dissolved, gradually bring the mixture to the boil. Once boiling, increase the heat and allow to boil vigorously for about 3 minutes, or until the cream has reduced by around 30 per cent.

Remove from the heat, allow the bubbles to briefly subside and add the citrus zests and juices. Whisk vigorously until well combined, then add the salt and whisk well once more.

Cover the mixture with a piece of baking parchment so that it touches the surface and leave to steep at room temperature for 20 minutes. Pass the mixture through a fine sieve into a jug, pressing it through with the back of a spoon or spatula to catch the zest.

Divide the mixture evenly between three small serving glasses or ramekins and transfer to the fridge to set for around 3 hours.

Meanwhile, prepare the shortbread. Combine the caster sugar, lime zest and butter in a bowl or stand mixer and beat together until pale and creamy.

In a separate bowl, combine the flour, ground almonds desiccated coconut and salt, and mix well.

Add the dry ingredients to the butter mixture and beat gently until the mixture just starts to clump together. Use your hand to bring the mixture into a rough dough and immediately wrap in cling film.

Gently roll the cling-filmed dough into an oval or rectangular disc and rest in the fridge for 30 minutes.

Once rested, roll out the dough between two pieces of baking parchment to around 5mm (¼in) thick. Stamp out biscuits using a 5–6cm (2–2¼in) cookie cutter – you should get about eight in total.

Place the biscuits on a baking tray lined with baking parchment, loosely cover with cling film or parchment and refrigerate for a further 30 minutes.

While the biscuit dough rests, prepare the blackberry compote. Combine the blackberries, caster sugar, lemon juice and bay leaf, if using, in a saucepan over a medium heat and bring to a boil. Simmer for 10–15 minutes, or until well reduced.

Pass through a sieve, pushing as much of the juices through as possible. Discard the pips and allow to cool, then cover and refrigerate until ready to serve.

Preheat the oven to 180°C/160°C fan/350°F/Gas 4. Bake the shortbread biscuits in the oven for about 14 minutes, or until golden. Remove from the oven and sprinkle with caster sugar, gently dusting off any excess before transferring to a wire rack to cool.

To serve, remove the set possets from the fridge, spoon over some of the blackberry compote and serve with a biscuit or two.

No-churn Ice Cream

I really think I should invest in an ice-cream machine because I do love a scoop of cold, creamy goodness. My good friend Becca and I chat at length about ice cream – notably our discovery of new flavours, and of course deliberating over our favourites – hers is rum and raisin, if you're wondering, but I'm more of a fruit ripple or cookie dough gal. I have vivid memories of eating a raspberry ripple gelato while on a holiday in Lake Garda... it was sublime.

Without an ice-cream machine, I have to get a bit creative. My favourite way to make ice cream at home is to use a combination of condensed milk and double cream which, when whipped up and frozen, creates a wonderfully scoopable 'ice cream' that can be flavoured as you choose.

Below I have provided a base vanilla recipe. It makes a lot, but uses up a whole tin of condensed milk – because who really wants half a tin of condensed milk lying around? Because of this, I have suggested halving the base mixture and pairing each half with two different flavourings.

Makes
about 1 litre (1¾ pints)

Hands-on time
35 minutes + minimum
6 hours freezing time

Cookie dough

55g (2¼oz) plain flour

60g (2½oz) unsalted butter

35g (1¼oz) caster sugar

20g (¾oz) soft light brown sugar

¼ tsp sea salt

1 tbsp sour cream

1 Daim bar (or your favourite chocolate), roughly chopped

Raspberry ripple

125g (4¼oz) raspberries (fresh or frozen)

30g (1¼oz) caster sugar

1 tsp lemon juice

Vanilla ice cream base

397g (14oz) tin condensed milk

¼–½ tsp sea salt

2 tsp lemon juice

2 tsp vanilla extract

550ml (20fl oz) double cream

First prepare the cookie dough. Preheat the oven to 180°C/160°C fan/350°F/Gas 4. Spread the flour onto a baking tray in an even layer and bake for 5–10 minutes to kill any bacteria. Leave to cool fully.

In a bowl, beat together the butter and sugars until well combined, add the salt and sour cream and beat again until homogenous. Add the cooled flour and stir through until just combined, then add the Daim bar or chocolate and stir until just incorporated.

Transfer to a loaf tin lined with baking parchment and level the top. Cover and place in the freezer to firm up. Once frozen, remove from the freezer and chop into small chunks. Return the cookie dough chunks to the freezer until ready to use.

Next, prepare the raspberry ripple. Combine the raspberries, sugar and lemon juice in a medium sized saucepan over a low-medium heat and stir until the sugar dissolves. Increase the heat to medium and simmer for 10–15 minutes, or until reduced and thickened. Pass through a sieve into a bowl and set aside to cool fully. Chill once cooled to room temperature.

For the vanilla ice cream base, place two airtight plastic containers in the freezer to chill. Combine the condensed milk, salt, lemon juice and vanilla extract in a bowl, stirring well to combine. Add the cream and beat until aerated, voluminous and forming stiff peaks.

To assemble, divide the vanilla base mixture evenly between two large bowls. Remove the plastic containers from the freezer. Remove the cookie dough chunks from the freezer and sprinkle them into one of the bowls of base mixture. Fold through until evenly distributed, then transfer to the container and level with a palette knife.

Dot about a quarter of the raspberry mixture over the bottom of the second container, then add a third of the remaining base mixture and gently level with a palette knife. Spoon over another quarter of the raspberry mixture, dotting it over the surface, and use a skewer to gently drag the raspberry mixture through the cream to create a ripple. Repeat with the remaining base and raspberry mixture until it is all used up.

Place both containers in the freezer and leave to set firm for a minimum of 6 hours – overnight is best. Scoop and serve as you wish.

Notes

Any fruit purée can be substituted here – if you choose a fruit like peach, peel it before weighing out to the specified amount. No need to sieve.

In place of the cookie dough, you could use chunks of chopped up brownie, honeycomb, your favourite chocolate bar, pretzels or nuts – it's time to get creative!

Brown Butter Rice Crispy Treats

Among many other aspects, I love the diversity of baking. You can spend hours, even days, labouring over pastry, bread or cakes and constructing multiple different elements, or you can simply throw together a few simple ingredients, and both yield an equally satisfying result. This bake is one of the latter types – simplicity to the max but an exceptional, perfectly balanced sweet treat. For me, rice crispy treats are synonymous with my childhood, often bought for 20p from the school tuck shop, sticky, sweet and inhaled at break time with a glass of milk.

My version draws on that nostalgia, with a little sophistication thrown in – I've browned the butter, and combined it with peanut butter for added nuttiness and flavour, and just in case there weren't enough nuts, I've added some roasted peanuts for texture. A combination of crisped rice cereal and oats are glued together with just enough marshmallow that they're not overly sweet and I've topped it all off with a salted caramel ganache – not entirely necessary, but a wonderful accompaniment to the crispy nutty layer nestled beneath.

Makes
16 squares

Hands-on time
20 minutes + 1 hour setting time

~~~~~~

60g (2½oz) unsalted butter

150g (5oz) white mini marshmallows

¼ tsp sea salt

50g (2oz) unsweetened smooth or crunchy peanut butter

100g (3½oz) crisped rice cereal

30g (1¼oz) rolled oats

50g (2oz) roasted peanuts, chopped

Salted caramel ganache

150g (5oz) milk or dark chocolate, chopped

80ml (3oz) double cream

¼ tsp vanilla extract

50g (2oz) caster sugar

5g (1 tsp) unsalted butter

Pinch of flaky sea salt, plus extra for sprinkling (optional)

Line a 20 x 20 cm (8 x 8in) baking tin with baking parchment. Make sure all your ingredients are measured out and ready, as you need to work quick quickly.

First prepare the brown butter. Melt the butter in a small saucepan over a medium heat, stirring frequently. It will melt then start to foam. When the foam subsides, it will begin to turn golden and start to smell nutty – when this happens, remove the butter from the heat and add the marshmallows and salt. Stir constantly until the marshmallows have almost melted then add the peanut butter and stir to combine until everything has melted together.

Working quickly, add the crisped rice cereal, oats and chopped nuts and stir until all the dry ingredients are coated in the sticky mixture. Immediately transfer to the prepared tin and use a second piece of baking parchment to press the mixture into the tin. Cool for 20 minutes, or until set.

Meanwhile, prepare the salted caramel ganache. Put the chocolate into a heatproof bowl and set aside until required. Gently heat the cream and vanilla extract in the microwave or in a saucepan placed over a low heat – just until it is warmed.

Pour the sugar into a clean saucepan over a medium heat and allow the sugar to melt until it turns a dark amber colour. Remove from the heat and add the butter and a pinch of salt, stirring to combine, then gradually add the warm cream, stirring continuously until smooth. Pour the hot caramel over the chocolate and leave to stand for a couple of minutes before stirring from the centre until a smooth ganache forms.

Pour the ganache over the rice crispy base, tilting the tin to encourage it to spread out evenly and form a smooth finish – alternatively, level with a palette knife. Once the ganache has cooled slightly, sprinkle over the optional flaky sea salt. Leave to set for 40 minutes before cutting into 16 small squares.

Notes

When making the salted caramel ganache, if the caramel is still extremely hot after you have added the cream, allow it to cool a little (90°C/194°F is optimal) before pouring over the chocolate – this prevents any risk of separation.

To clean the caramel pan, fill it with boiling water and set over a medium heat. This will help to melt the sticky mixture from the base and sides.

Full-on Joy

For me, the feelings of adventure, intrigue and excitement
remain fundamental to baking, however long you've been doing it. Baking can be unpredictable at times and mistakes can happen, but when approached with a curious mind and a kind heart, there is always joy to be had. We are conditioned from a young age to pass exams, 'be successful' and achieve, but this doesn't prepare us for misfortune or challenges. Baking provides an excellent medium through which to explore the world as if we were children again – it is a lesson in getting things a bit wrong and learning from our mistakes, but not being defeated by them. There is always more knowledge to acquire, so the incentive never wanes.

Arguably the most life-affirming acts are those that make others feel loved and appreciated. Besides all the personal gains we experience when baking, sharing our favourite bakes with others (either as a gift or as part of our jobs), can heighten our overall sense of well-being. On a personal level, we feel that we have done something good for the world, which in turn can give our lives meaning and help us feel more connected to others. The resulting lift in our mood – the happiness, optimism and boost to our confidence – can also be felt by those around us. And it doesn't stop there, as many will in turn feel encouraged to repeat a good deed that they have experienced – ripples of joy spread out into the world generating a more positive community. It's remarkable to think that a humble cupcake can be a catalyst for such happiness.

The definition of a joyful bake is once again personal. For me, it's not limited to sweet or savoury, it's not a particular genre of baking and speed is not a factor, instead, it is governed by the preferences of the people I have in mind to receive it. It can be anything from simple cheese scones or rustic bread rolls to enjoy at home with Mum – any bread and cheese product goes down well in our house – to a showstopping tropical cake for a friend's birthday or a comforting custard tart to share with neighbours. The reward for me is unwavering, and the appreciation from others is yet another boost to my confidence.

Baking may not be able to provide the answers to all of life's problems, but having benefited so much from its magical powers, I feel passionate about highlighting the happiness there is to be found in it and the psychological advantages that can be gained. I hope that some of the bakes in the following chapter provide you with joy – failing that, I would encourage you to seek out your ultimate bakes (or if it isn't baking, your ultimate passions), pursue them unreservedly and witness positivity and happiness flow into your life and the lives of the people you touch.

Rustic Mediterranean Rolls

Makes
12 rolls
Hands-on time
25 minutes + 3¾ hours
proving and resting
time
Cooking time
20 minutes

I visited Rome in 2017 and it was undoubtedly one of my favourite holidays, largely due to the food scene – the architecture and history is unbelievable but, in my opinion, the carbs on offer trump all of that. The carbonara, pizza, gelato and coffee I ate and drank were second to none. My most vivid memory, however, is of the artfully simplistic yet tantalizingly flavoursome sandwiches I picked up from back-street cafés – they were out of this world. I was blown away by these humble lunchtime offerings, comprised of just a few quality ingredients. My favourite was a ciabatta drizzled with a little oil, stuffed with roasted peppers, aubergine and courgette, layered with premium mozzarella and finished with more oil and a scattering of basil leaves.

These rolls are an ode to my Roman adventure. Gnarly, irregularly shaped, with a crisp yet tender crust and an open crumb, they are the perfect vehicle for all manner of sandwich fillings.

400g (14oz) strong white bread flour

70g (2¾oz) wholemeal bread flour

30g (1¼oz) spelt flour

10g (¼oz) fast-action dried yeast

10g (¼oz) sea salt

400ml (14fl oz) tepid water

Olive oil, for greasing

Flavourings

100g (3½oz) pitted black pitted olives, drained and patted dry then roughly chopped

50g (2oz) sun-dried tomatoes, drained and patted dry then chopped

100g (3½oz) feta, drained and patted dry then diced

Combine the flours in a large bowl, then add the yeast to one side of the bowl and the salt to the other. Add the tepid water and use a wooden spoon to bring together into a sticky dough. Cover and leave to autolyse at room temperature for 20–30 minutes.

Knead the dough either in a stand mixer on a medium setting or by hand for 12–15 minutes. It is a very wet dough, so if kneading by hand see Notes opposite. After 15 minutes, cover again and leave the dough to rest for a further 10 minutes.

Once rested, knead the dough for a further 2 minutes. It should now be very elastic and visibly smoother, pulling away from the sides of the bowl. Add the flavourings: start with the olives and tomatoes and briefly knead them into the dough for 2–3 minutes, then follow up with the feta, lightly kneading to incorporate.

Once everything is combined, transfer the dough to a lightly oiled deep container or bowl and leave to prove somewhere warm for 2 hours.

Notes

This dough is very wet, but it is possible to knead by hand using either the slap and fold technique or the Rubaud method. For a wonderful explanation of hand-kneading wet doughs like this, I thoroughly recommend the website The Perfect Loaf – Maurizio provides loads of information, recipes, videos and pictures to explain the various kneading techniques in more detail and when to implement them. He mainly focuses on sourdough, but this high-hydration recipe is similar in concept, so head there for some extra tips on kneading.

Using a baking stone to bake these rolls will yield great results. If you have one, pop it in the oven while it heats up then carefully slide the dough balls (with their parchment) onto the stone to bake.

If you don't add in the extras, these are epic served with a drizzle of extra virgin olive oil, creamy whipped ricotta cheese and either blistered tomatoes and balsamic vinegar or honey-glazed figs.

After 30 minutes of proving time, perform a quick 'stretch and fold' of the dough. Use a wet hand to scoop under the dough, lift it up and gently stretch it until you feel some resistance, then fold it over itself. Rotate the bowl 90 degrees and repeat. Do this twice more so you have performed a total of four folds. Cover again and leave to finish proving.

Line two large baking trays with baking parchment. Use a floured dough scraper to gently release the dough from the sides of the container, before turning out onto a floured work surface.

Using a well-floured dough scraper or a very sharp knife, cut the dough into 12 chunks and place them onto the prepared baking trays. Cover and prove for a further 45–60 minutes.

Meanwhile, preheat the oven to 240°C/220°C fan/475°F/Gas 9. Once the rolls have had their second prove (they will seem horribly flat, but don't panic) transfer them to the oven and bake for 20 minutes. Once baked, remove from the oven and leave to cool on a wire rack.

Cheese 'n' Spice Scones

If you hadn't already gathered, I'm a fan of all things cheese. In my first book, *The Joy of Baking*, I gave you my grandma's cheese 'n' spice biscuits and they seemed to be quite a hit with people (I can't argue – Grandma was a legend). It got me thinking about whether I could pimp a scone with the same epic flavour pairing.

Fundamental to this bake was ensuring the cheesy flavour sang, so I've gone extra-strong, with Cheddar and Parmesan in fairly large quantities. I've also suggested a little extra cheese to top them with, because there can never too much cheese, right? The spice is enough to be detectable but doesn't overpower the cheese and the scones are light and airy with the addition of buttermilk to the dough – it's a marriage made in heaven.

Makes
6–8 scones

Hands-on time
15 minutes +
20 minutes resting time

Cooking time
15 minutes

Preheat the oven to 200°C/180°C fan/400°F/Gas 6 and place a baking tray inside to preheat.

Combine the flour, baking powder, salt and cayenne pepper in a large bowl and briefly mix to combine. Rub the butter into the flour until it resembles coarse breadcrumbs.

Add the cheeses and gently toss to combine. Add the buttermilk and use a knife to cut through the mixture, eventually using your hand to bring it together into a rough dough.

Transfer to the work surface and very gently knead the dough a couple of times. Roll out the dough to about 2.5cm (1in) thick and then use a 5–6cm (2–2¼in) cookie cutter dredged in plain flour to stamp out rounds. Transfer to a plate or another baking tray and place in the fridge to rest for 20 minutes.

Remove the scones from the fridge, brush with the egg yolk and sprinkle with the additional Cheddar. Remove the preheated baking tray from the oven, quickly top with baking parchment and place the scones on the tray, spaced slightly apart. Bake for 15–20 minutes, or until golden brown. Remove the baked scones from the oven and transfer to a wire rack to cool, covering with a tea towel to help keep them most.

200g (7oz) plain flour

2½ tsp baking powder

½ tsp fine sea salt

½ tsp cayenne pepper

55g (2¼oz) cold unsalted
butter, cubed

60g (2½oz) extra-mature
Cheddar, coarsely grated

40g (1½oz) Parmesan,
finely grated

135ml (4¾fl oz) buttermilk

Topping

1 egg yolk, lightly beaten

20g (¾oz) extra-mature
Cheddar, finely grated

Notes

These scones are still great on the second day if given a 10-second zap in the microwave. They're also great to freeze and enjoy at a later date.

This recipe is easy to adapt for different flavour combinations – try cheese and chive, Marmite and cheese, or harissa and Manchego, or add a handful of sun-dried tomatoes and basil to the mix. Swap in different cheeses, too – crumbled Stilton, pecorino or Gruyère would all work. Just make sure the cheese is nice and strong.

Cauliflower Cheese Soufflé

Serves
2–3

Hands-on time
20 minutes

Cooking time
25–30 minutes

Anyone who followed my *Great British Bake Off* journey may well laugh at the sight of a cheese soufflé recipe – I had to make a twice-baked souffle in the final and it was an epic failure. I vowed never to bother with one of these monsters again but then, a whole 24 months later, I stumbled across my great grandmother's old recipe book and found a recipe for 'Easy Cheese Soufflé'. I was lured in by the 'easy' part and figured it was time to face my demons once more and give cheese soufflés a second chance. The result? Well, let's just say Great Grandma Rosie was clearly a bit of a legend.

Firstly, it was indeed fairly straightforward, and a little rustic, which I liked, but more importantly, it was heavenly – rich yet airy and light, cheesy, comforting and warming. Having baked it twice in a few days, I tried it again, this time with a few tweaks of my own – I added par-cooked cauliflower and English mustard, and opted for Gruyère over Cheddar due to its wonderful nuttiness. These changes aren't essential, simplicity works here, but they add another subtle flavour dimension which really complements this already great bake.

120g (4oz) cauliflower, cut into small-medium florets

30g (1¼oz) unsalted butter, plus extra for greasing

15g (1 tbsp) plain flour, plus extra for dusting

140ml (4¾fl oz) whole milk, warmed

1 tsp English mustard

110g (3¾oz) Gruyère cheese, grated

3 large eggs, separated

Sea salt and black pepper

Notes

Any leftovers can be enjoyed cold the next day.

Switch up the veg and try kale or broccoli or add a little leek too.

Try some nutmeg grated into the sauce for an extra flavour dimension.

Preheat the oven to 190°C/170°C fan/375°F/Gas 5. Grease a 15cm (6in) dish with deep sides (about 10cm/4in) with butter and lightly dust with flour.

Place the cauliflower florets in a microwave-safe dish and cook in the microwave on full power for 2½–3 minutes – the cauliflower should be almost tender but still fairly firm. (Alternatively, steam or par-boil the cauliflower – if par-boiled, drain thoroughly and pat dry with kitchen paper to remove any excess moisture.) Set aside to cool.

Next prepare the white sauce; melt the butter in a saucepan over a medium heat, add the flour and whisk to form a roux. Slowly add the warmed milk, whisking continuously. Once all the milk has been added, continue to cook for 5 minutes over a medium-low heat, still stirring continuously, to cook out the flour. Season with salt and pepper and stir in the mustard. Remove the mixture from the heat and stir through the cheese, allowing it to melt a little.

Allow the mixture to cool a little before whisking in the egg yolks, one at a time. Once all the egg yolks have been added, set aside.

Arrange the cooled cauliflower evenly in the base of your dish. Next whisk the egg whites to medium-soft peaks, add a spoonful to the cheesy sauce mixture and beat in to loosen a little, then fold in the remaining egg whites in three stages, taking care not to knock out too much air.

Pour the prepared mixture into the dish, on top of the cauliflower florets – take care to not knock out the air as you transfer it.

Bake for 25–30 minutes, or until risen and golden and a skewer inserted into the soufflé comes out virtually clean. Serve immediately.

Blackberry and Roasted Almond Blondies

Makes
16 squares

Hands-on time
15–20 minutes

Cooking time
55–60 minutes

I'm not really a big blondie fan, but despite this, when compiling recipes for this book, I became slightly obsessed with the idea that a blondie recipe had to make the line-up. As you may have gathered, I'm not one for sickly sweet bakes. I like things that have depth and complexity – in my eyes, sweetness always needs to be tempered with something salty, toasty, fruity or tart. So, to say this recipe caused me some head-scratching would be an understatement.

People often say blondies are one of the easiest things to bake – well, I managed to prove them wrong. Raw, greasy, overbaked on top, too sweet, seized chocolate... you name it, I encountered it. However, with some persistence, I have hit the jackpot. This is my version of magnificent. Critics may argue that it's baked too much for a blondie, or lacking in tooth-aching sweetness, but I think what I have created here really works. It's gooey in the centre but the outside pieces have a little more bite; it's nutty and balanced with salt; and it's really brought to life with the addition of blackberries. Blondie fan or not, I think this one might just convert you.

75g (2¾oz) blanched almonds

165g (5¾oz) unsalted butter

225g (8oz) good-quality white chocolate, roughly chopped

85g (3oz) plain flour

75g (2¾oz) spelt flour

6g (¾ tsp) sea salt

3 large eggs

135g (4¾oz) soft light brown sugar

90g (3¼oz) golden caster sugar

100g (3½oz) frozen blackberries, halved if large

15g (½oz) flaked almonds

Cream, to serve (optional)

Preheat the oven to 180°C/160°C fan/350°F/Gas 4. Grease a 20cm (8in) square baking tin and line with baking parchment

Pour the blanched almonds onto a baking tray and roast in the oven for around 10 minutes, or until lightly browned. Remove from the oven and set aside to cool before roughly chopping.

Pour 2.5cm (1in) water into a small saucepan over a medium heat and bring to a simmer. Meanwhile, put the butter and white chocolate into a large heatproof bowl. Once the water is simmering, turn off the heat and place the bowl of chocolate and butter over the pan, ensuring the bottom of the bowl doesn't touch the water. Stir periodically as the two gently melt together. Alternatively, you can do this in the microwave, heating in short intervals. Once completely melted, set the mixture aside to cool a little while you prepare the remaining ingredients.

Notes

Be careful when melting the chocolate and butter as white chocolate is notoriously fragile when heated and when 'contaminated' with water – I discovered this the hard way, which is both messy and expensive if you end up working your way through 750g (1½lb) white chocolate repeating the same mistake.

If your chocolate does split, there is a little trick you can employ (thank you to my good friend Becca for this top tip). Add a dribble of whole milk and blend with an immersion blender.

If you struggle to find blackberries or they're not in season, try raspberries – they're not quite as tart, but still a worthy alternative.

Sift the flours and salt into a bowl. Crack the eggs into another large bowl and briefly whisk together with the two sugars until homogenous and slightly aerated (don't overmix).

Once the butter and chocolate mixture has cooled a bit, pour it into the sugar and egg mixture and beat to combine. Add the flours and chopped almonds and gently fold into the mixture – don't overwork the batter or the blondie will be tough.

Transfer the batter to the prepared baking tin and level with a palette knife or the back of a spatula, then gently press the blackberries into the top of the batter and sprinkle over the flaked almonds. Bake in the oven for 55–60 minutes.

Remove from the oven and allow to cool completely in the tin before cutting into 16 pieces. They're wonderful as they are, or heated briefly in the microwave and served with a drizzle of cream.

Chocolate and Cherry Swiss Roll with Almond Brittle

I have a confession to make – I hadn't made a Swiss roll prior to developing this recipe. Then why include it in the book, you ask? Simple: because of Colin. That's Colin the Caterpillar, to be clear. I assume it's just a British thing, but Colin is the chocolate sponge birthday cake that fulfils every child's (and adult's, who are we kidding?) birthday dream.

    I knew I couldn't possibly match the heady heights of Colin but was compelled to generate a little ode to him here. The sponge is airy and light, the filling fresh and creamy and paired with some insanely flavourful cherries, and the whole thing is covered in a whipped chocolate ganache and almond brittle for crunch. OK, so it isn't Colin, but it does taste great. Perfect as a Christmas dessert, birthday cake or just because you fancy it.

Serves
8–10

Hands-on time
45 minutes

Cooking time
20–23 minutes

40g (1½oz) cocoa powder

1 tsp espresso powder

Pinch of sea salt

5 large eggs, separated

125g (4¼oz) caster sugar

1 tsp whole milk

1 tbsp icing sugar, sifted, for dusting

Fresh cherries, to garnish

Almond brittle

75g (2¾oz) caster sugar

1 tbsp water

1 tsp unsalted butter

35g (1¼ oz) flaked almonds, toasted

Cherry filling

200g (7oz) frozen cherries, defrosted and drained

15g (½oz) caster sugar

Squeeze of lemon juice

¼ tsp almond extract

1 tsp kirsch (optional)

1 tsp cornflour

Ganache topping

100g (3½oz) dark chocolate, roughly chopped

50ml (2fl oz) double cream

75g (2¾oz) unsalted butter

Chantilly cream filling

200ml (7fl oz) double cream

1 tbsp icing sugar

1 tbsp kirsch (optional)

First make the almond brittle. Line a baking tray with baking parchment. Put the sugar and water into a heavy-based saucepan over a low heat and swirl gently until the sugar has dissolved. Once the sugar has dissolved, increase the heat to medium and bring to a simmer. Once bubbling and a dark amber colour, add the butter and stir with a lightly greased spatula to combine.

Remove from the heat and add the almonds, briefly stirring to coat before pouring out onto the prepared baking tray. Working quickly, spread the mixture out as evenly as you can using the back of the spatula before leaving to cool.

Next, prepare the cherry filling. Combine the drained cherries with the sugar, lemon juice, almond extract and Kirsch, if using, in a saucepan. Stir and leave to macerate for a minimum of 30 minutes, or overnight. Once macerated, add the cornflour to the mixture and stir to combine. Place the mixture over a medium heat, stirring continuously, until the liquid syrup thickens. Transfer to a bowl and allow to cool completely.

Prepare the sponge. Preheat the oven to 180°C/160°C fan/350°F/Gas 4. Grease a 23 x 33cm (9 x 13in) Swiss roll tin with baking parchment.

Sift together the cocoa powder, espresso powder and salt into a bowl. Using an electric hand mixer, whisk the egg yolks and 85g (3oz) of the caster sugar on medium-high speed for around 3 minutes, or until thicker, pale and increased in volume. Add the sifted cocoa powder mixture, folding to combine, then finally add the milk and fold in. Set aside while you prepare the egg whites.

In a clean bowl with a clean whisk attachment, whisk the egg whites on medium speed. Once pale and frothy, add the remaining caster sugar, 1 teaspoon at a time, allowing it to incorporate before each further addition. Continue to whisk until you have medium-stiff peaks. Add the egg white mixture to the yolk mixture in three stages, gently folding through until streak-free.

Pour the batter into the prepared tin, level with a spatula and bake in the oven for 20–23 minutes, or until risen and springy to the touch and a skewer inserted into the cake comes out clean.

Once baked, remove from the oven, line a wire rack with a clean tea towel and sprinkle over the sifted icing sugar, then turn the sponge out

Notes

Once baked and removed from the oven, the sponge has a tendency to shrink away from the tin and 'deflate' a little. Don't be put off by this, it's quite normal.

Don't feel limited by the flavour pairing here. Use brandy, Grand Marnier or Baileys in the cream, or use a different kind of berry for the filling. Or, if chocolate is your preference, double up on the chocolate ganache topping and use half for the filling.

onto the tea towel and remove the baking parchment. While still warm, roll the sponge up from one of the shorter sides with the tea towel still inside. Leave to cool fully.

Meanwhile, prepare the ganache. Combine the chocolate, cream and butter in a heatproof bowl over a pan of simmering water and stir until a smooth, glossy mixture forms. Remove from the heat and set aside to cool and thicken to a spreadable consistency. Once cooled, use an electric hand mixer to whip it until lighter in colour and slightly increased in volume.

For the Chantilly cream filling, beat together the double cream, icing sugar and kirsch, if using, until it holds soft peaks.

To assemble, carefully unfurl the rolled-up sponge, remove the tea towel and spread a layer of Chantilly cream over the cooled cake, leaving a 2cm (¾in) border at both the short ends. Distribute the cherries and their sticky syrup evenly over the cream. Roll back up into a log.

Transfer the cake to a serving platter and spread the thickened chocolate ganache over the cake, adding texture with the palette knife. Crush the brittle or break into shards and sprinkle over the top of the cake, interspersed with cherries, before refrigerating for a minimum of 15–20 minutes to slightly firm up before serving.

Coconut, Passion Fruit and Rum Cake

When I was nine, Mum and I went with my grandma and her friends, Maxine and Tia, to Cuba. One of my lasting memories from that holiday was drinking piña colada cocktails in the sea (not strictly for me at the time but I seemed to hang off Mum's straw!). This cake captures that memory for me. It briefly whisks me off to the Caribbean, cocktail in hand, crystal blue waters and white sandy beaches in front of me.

I have opted for passion fruit over pineapple for the curd filling as I find it brings a more fruity, tropical vibe. The coconut-cream cake is light, fluffy and oh-so moist and the luxurious Swiss meringue buttercream is a perfect rich balance to the natural sweetness from the curd and cake. It's all spiked with (optional) rum, which adds a little element of naughtiness to this magical cake.

Serves
12

Hands-on time
1 hour 20 minutes

Cooking time
25 minutes + cooling time

~~~~~~~~~~~~~~~~~~~~~~~~~~~~

50g (2oz) coconut cream

60ml (2½fl oz) whole milk

60g (2½oz) desiccated coconut

½ tsp coconut extract

250g (9oz) unsalted butter, softened

250g (9oz) caster sugar

4 large eggs

250g (9oz) plain flour

3 tsp baking powder

Pinch of sea salt

Rum syrup

50g (2oz) caster sugar

Zest of ½ lime

50ml (2fl oz) water

2 tbsp dark rum

Passion fruit and lime curd

3 large egg yolks (reserve the whites for the frosting)

1 large egg

9 large passion fruit

15ml (1 tbsp) lime juice

75g (2¾oz) caster sugar

90g (3¼oz) unsalted butter

Swiss meringue buttercream

3 egg whites (reserved from the curd)

220g (7½oz) caster sugar

330g (11½oz) unsalted butter, at room temperature, diced

3 tbsp Malibu or white rum

Decoration

Handful of toasted coconut chips

1 passion fruit

Preheat the oven to 180°C/160°C fan/350°F/Gas 4. Grease four 18cm (6in) round cake tins and line with baking parchment.

Combine the coconut cream and milk in a saucepan and warm gently over a low heat (or microwave on full power for 20 seconds). Add the desiccated coconut and coconut extract and stir to combine, then leave to steep while you prepare the remaining ingredients.

Combine the butter and sugar in a large bowl or the bowl of a stand mixer and beat on a medium speed for about 5 minutes until very pale, light, fluffy and increased in volume. Next add the eggs one at a time, beating thoroughly between each addition.

Sift together the flour, baking powder and salt in a large bowl then fold into the wet ingredients, alternating with the milk and coconut mixture until smooth.

Divide the cake batter evenly between the prepared tins and bake for 20–25 minutes, or until risen, golden and a skewer inserted into the cakes comes out clean.

While the cakes bake, prepare the syrup. Combine the sugar, lime zest and water in a small saucepan over a low heat. Once the sugar has dissolved, increase the heat to medium, bring to the boil and simmer for 1 minute before removing from the heat. Add the rum and stir to combine. Set aside to cool.

For the curd, lightly whisk the egg yolks with the whole egg and set aside. Scoop the pulp and seeds out of the passion fruit and place in a small food processor or high-speed blender and pulse several times to release the pulp from the seeds. Pass the mixture through a sieve, discarding the seeds.

Notes

If you want to simplify this recipe, you could buy a passion fruit curd and whip up a simple American rum buttercream instead of making the Swiss meringue version. Simply beat 225g (8oz) softened unsalted butter until light and fluffy, then add 400g (14oz) sifted icing sugar in three stages followed by 3 tablespoons white rum.

Surplus passion fruit curd can be kept in the fridge for 1–2 weeks and used for toast or to make Passion Fruit and Dark Chocolate Profiteroles (see page 86).

Measure out 180g (6¼oz) passion fruit juice and transfer to a heatproof bowl. Add the lime juice, caster sugar and butter. Place the bowl over a pan of gently simmering water and stir, allowing the butter to melt and the sugar to dissolve.

Once melted together, remove from the heat and slowly pour in the egg mixture, whisking continuously. Return the bowl to the pan of simmering water and whisk continuously for 15 minutes, or until the curd thickens. Transfer to a bowl (passing through a sieve if desired) and leave to cool.

For the buttercream, combine the egg whites and caster sugar in a clean, heatproof bowl. Place over a pan of gently simmering water and stir until the mixture reaches 60°C (140°F) on a sugar thermometer. Remove from the heat and, using an electric hand mixer, whisk for 8–10 minutes until the mixture is at room temperature.

Slowly start to add the butter, one piece at a time. Once it has all been added, continue to whisk until the mixture is smooth and silky. With the mixer still running, gradually add the rum, if using, and beat to combine.

To assemble, prepare the cake layers by levelling the tops of each sponge using a cake leveller or sharp knife. Brush each layer of cake generously with the rum syrup. Place a little of the frosting in the centre of a cake board or plate and add the first cake layer, then spread over a layer of the frosting followed by a generous portion of the passion fruit curd filling. Add the next cake layer and repeat.

Flip the final layer so that the flat bottom becomes the top of the cake. Apply a crumb coat of frosting to the top and sides of the cake and refrigerate for 30–60 minutes to firm up.

Once the frosting is 'dry' to the touch, remove the cake from the fridge and apply a top coat of frosting. Roughly smooth before using a palette knife to dab the wet buttercream, creating a stucco effect.

Next, pipe a few buttercream stars on top of the cake in a crescent shape, dot on a few blobs of passion fruit curd and finish with a few sprinkles of toasted coconut, all following the same crescent. Place a halved passion fruit on top of the cake, scooping out a little flesh to drizzle between the piped buttercream. Eat immediately or refrigerate until you intend to serve the cake.

Baked Apple Crumble and Custard Cheesecake Squares

I'm that person, who, when presented with the dessert menu, finds it too much pressure to choose. I play the tactical, 'let's all share' card, with the sole intention of making sure I get a sample of everything I fancy. This recipe aims to take care of this problem by combining two of the greatest desserts into one – resourceful, I think. Crumble and cheesecake must be two of the best desserts of all time: simple, unpretentious and comforting.

When it comes to crumble, orchard fruits are my go-to, with apple arguably the finest. As for the crumble itself, it must contain nuts and some good nuggety clusters, and it must be sufficiently rich with butter to balance the sweetness. Meanwhile, where cheesecake is concerned, I'm easily pleased – vanilla is my preference, paired with a generously thick buttery biscuit base. This recipe unites the best of these two concepts, with a biscuit base topped with a tangy vanilla cheesecake mix, rippled with a rich apple compote and topped with a lightly spiced pecan crumble. It's comforting, sweet – yet not cloyingly so – and wholesome.

Makes
16 squares

Hands-on time
30 minutes + 5 hours chilling time

Cooking time
1 hour 20 minutes

Biscuit base

200g (7oz) digestive biscuits

Pinch of sea salt

80g (3oz) unsalted butter, melted

Apple compote

45g (1¾oz) unsalted butter

300g (11oz) peeled and diced Bramley apple flesh (from about 1 large apple)

45g (1¾oz) soft light brown sugar

¼ tsp vanilla extract

Squeeze of lemon juice

Pinch of sea salt

Crumble topping

70g (2¾oz) plain flour

50g (2oz) cold unsalted butter, cubed

20g (¾oz) soft light brown sugar

15g (½oz) caster sugar

½ tsp ground cinnamon

Pinch of sea salt

40g (1½oz) pecans, finely chopped

Cheesecake

290g (10¼oz) full-fat cream cheese

60g (2½oz) sour cream

95g (3¼oz) caster sugar

1 large egg

¼ tsp sea salt

1 tsp vanilla extract

10g (¼oz) cornflour

First prepare the biscuit base. Preheat the oven to 180°C/160°C fan/350°F/Gas 4. Grease a 20 x 20cm (8 x 8in) square tin and line with baking parchment.

Combine the digestive biscuits and salt in a food processor and blitz to a fine crumb (alternatively, place in a bag and bash with a rolling pin). Add the butter and pulse until it resembles wet sand. Transfer to the tin and press the mixture gently to form an even layer. Bake for 15 minutes, or until golden brown. Once baked, allow to cool completely.

Meanwhile, prepare the apple compote. Melt the butter in a saucepan over a medium-low heat. Once melted, add the apples, sugar, vanilla extract, lemon juice and salt. Stir well to combine. Cook for 30 minutes, stirring frequently and breaking down the apples with the back of your spoon or spatula, until it has completely reduced to a thick purée. Once cooked, blitz in a food processor for an ultra-smooth texture if you like. Set aside to cool until ready to use.

For the crumble topping, combine the flour, butter, sugars, cinnamon and salt in a food processor and pulse to a fine crumb (alternatively, rub the butter into the dry ingredients by hand until it is a mealy consistency).

Transfer to a bowl, add the finely chopped pecans and mix to combine. Next use your hands to 'clump' the dough together a bit – as the butter softens, continue to scrunch the dough in your hands until the mixture is comprised of irregularly sized nuggets. Refrigerate until ready to use.

Finally, prepare the cheesecake filling. Put all the ingredients into a bowl and mix together until smooth and evenly combined. Pour the filling over the biscuit base and level with a palette knife.

Transfer 150g (5oz) of the apple compote to a piping bag (reserve any excess for your morning porridge!) and pipe over the cheesecake base – it doesn't need to look pretty. Use a skewer to swirl the compote into the cheesecake batter. Finally, scatter the crumble over the top before transferring it to the oven and baking for 30–35 minutes, or until the crumble is lightly browned on top.

Once baked, remove from the oven and allow to cool for 1 hour at room temperature before transferring to the fridge to chill completely for 4 hours, or overnight. Once cooled, cut into squares.

Note

This recipe could be made with almost any fruit – just make sure that it's not too watery or the cheesecake will struggle to set.

Sticky Fig, Coffee and Hazelnut Cake

Serves
12–14

Hands-on time
45 minutes + 1 hour soaking time

Bake time
25–30 minutes

I find it hard to get excited about autumn – all I can think of is darker mornings and evenings, the weather turning (cold and wet are not my vibe) and the impending gloominess of winter (ever the optimist, I know). However, it seems that my dear friend, food, is able to lift my spirits somewhat, with the ingredients that flourish at this time of year. In my opinion, figs are an underrated fruit, jammy-sweet and an absolute marvel in appearance.

In this cake, I have paired them with my other true loves: coffee, toasted hazelnuts and a hint of spice. Topped off with the subtle tang of one of my favourite frostings, a cinnamon ermine frosting (if you haven't heard of this, it's a game changer, I assure you), and smooth caramel, this cake is sophistication and comfort itself. This cake is a guaranteed autumnal mood booster.

65g (2½oz) dried figs, chopped into small pieces

75ml (2¾fl oz) strong brewed coffee

75g (2¾oz) blanched hazelnuts, toasted

200g (7oz) self-raising flour

½ tsp bicarbonate of soda

¼ tsp fine sea salt

2 tsp mixed spice

50ml (2oz) buttermilk

2 tsp vanilla extract

200g (7oz) unsalted butter, softened

225g (8oz) soft light brown sugar

4 large eggs

Cinnamon ermine frosting

40g (1½oz) plain flour

140g (4¾oz) caster sugar

½ tsp fine sea salt

240ml (8fl ½oz) buttermilk

240g (8½oz) unsalted butter

2 tsp vanilla extract

¾–1 tsp ground cinnamon

Caramel

40ml (1½fl oz) water

75g (2¾oz) caster sugar

85ml (3fl oz) double cream, lukewarm

½ tsp vanilla extract

Pinch of sea salt

Decoration

Handful of toasted hazelnuts, chopped

3–4 small fresh figs

Put the figs into a bowl, cover with the coffee and leave for 30–60 minutes to soak. Preheat the oven to 180°C/160°C fan/350°F/Gas 4, grease four 15cm (6in) round cake tins and line with baking parchment.

Pulse the hazelnuts in a food processor until finely ground – don't overdo it or the oils will release from the nuts. Transfer to a small bowl until ready to use.

Sift the flour, bicarbonate of soda, salt and mixed spice into a large bowl and gently mix to combine. Add the hazelnuts, mix again, then set aside.

Once the figs have soaked, blitz to a smooth-ish paste in a food processor, transfer to a small bowl and stir in the buttermilk and vanilla extract, then set aside.

Meanwhile, beat the butter and sugar, either with an electric hand mixer or stand mixer, until pale, light and fluffy – be patient here, you really want to aerate the mixture.

Crack the eggs into a bowl and briefly whisk together. Once the butter and sugar are beaten, add the eggs a little at a time, ensuring each addition is incorporated before adding the next.

Once all the egg has been added, fold the flour/hazelnut mixture into the wet ingredients in three stages, alternating with the fig mixture – it is important not to overwork the mixture at this stage or you'll end up with a dense cake.

Divide the mixture between the cake tins – it should be about 260–270g (9¼–9½oz) batter per tin. Bake the cakes for 25–30 minutes, or until a skewer inserted into the centre comes out clean. Once baked, leave to stand in the tins for 5 minutes before turning out onto a wire rack to cool.

Next, prepare the roux for the frosting. Combine the flour, sugar and salt in a medium saucepan and gently whisk to combine. Add the buttermilk and whisk to a smooth consistency. Place over a medium-low heat and slowly bring to the boil, continually stirring with a small hand whisk.

Once the mixture starts to thicken, continue to whisk until it becomes a thick paste – a spoon dragged through the middle of the mixture should leave a line that gradually disappears over a few seconds. Transfer to a bowl and press a piece of cling film against the surface of the mixture to prevent a skin from forming. Leave at room temperature until completely cool.

While the cakes and roux are cooling, make the caramel. Combine the water and sugar in a saucepan over a medium heat. Leave until it turns a deep amber colour, then remove from the heat and carefully add the lukewarm cream a little at a time, stirring constantly. Once all the cream has been added, add the vanilla extract and salt. Transfer to a heatproof bowl and set aside to cool.

Once the roux has cooled, finish the frosting. Beat the butter with an electric hand whisk or in a stand mixer for 5–10 minutes until light, pale and fluffy. Add the cooled roux 1 tablespoon at a time, beating thoroughly between each addition. Once all the roux has been incorporated, add the vanilla and ground cinnamon to taste. Beat a final time to combine and set aside, covered, until ready to use.

To assemble the cake, first trim any doming from the top of each cake layer using a sharp serrated knife.

Next, place the first layer on a cake board, add a dollop of the frosting and smooth using a palette knife, then add the next cake layer and repeat with a layer of frosting before adding the final cake layer (flip this layer so that the flat bottom becomes the top). Ensure the cake is neatly layered and straight before adding a thin crumb coat of the frosting around the sides and top.

Transfer to the fridge to chill for 30–60 minutes. Once chilled, add a second thin coat of frosting to the top and sides of the cake, smoothing with a cake scraper.

Decorate with a caramel drip around the top circumference of the cake before spreading a thin layer of caramel over the entire top surface, then arrange the fresh figs in the centre of the cake and scatter over the toasted hazelnuts. Serve with any extra frosting and caramel.

Notes

The frosting and caramel recipes yield more than you need for the cake, so they can be served as an accompaniment or used on other bakes. The caramel can be kept in a sterilized jar for up to 2 weeks in the fridge – warm slightly before serving.

You can get as fancy as you like with the decoration. Add sprigs of rosemary or foliage for a truly autumnal vibe, or try dipping the toasted hazelnuts in a hard caramel before use.

To toast the hazelnuts, pop them in the oven at 180°C/160°C fan/350°F/Gas 4 for 10–15 minutes, or until lightly golden and aromatic.

German Pancakes with Lemon and Blueberry Compote

This is my answer to Pancake Day. I've pretended to like pancakes for a while, yet each year Pancake Day creeps up on me, I feel obliged to conform and inevitably I create something that is fine, but ultimately a little underwhelming. That was until I was enlightened by another of my Great Grandma Rosie's delicacies – German pancakes. Mum recalls fond memories of them enjoying supper together – it always featured pudding – and this was one of their favourites. Simple yet seemingly majestic, it's comforting and light all in one. I've paired Rosie's simple lemon-infused batter with a lemon and blueberry compote and some tangy sour cream.

Serves
4

Hands-on time
20 minutes

Cooking time
15–18 minutes +
30 minutes resting time

Combine the flour, salt and sugar in a large bowl, make a well in the middle and add the eggs and milk. Use a large whisk to beat the eggs into the milk, gradually incorporating the flour until a smooth liquid batter forms.

Add the lemon zest and stir to incorporate. Refrigerate for a minimum of 30 minutes.

Meanwhile, preheat the oven to 220°C/200°C fan/425°F/Gas 7. Pour a teaspoon of vegetable oil into each hole of a four-hole Yorkshire pudding tin (or use a deep muffin pan, but the cooking time may vary slightly). Place in the oven to get nice and hot.

When the batter has rested, remove it from the fridge and carefully remove the hot tin from the oven.

Evenly distribute the batter among the holes of the tin and quickly return to the oven for 15–18 minutes, or until puffed up and browned.

65g (2½oz) plain flour
Pinch of sea salt
2 tsp caster sugar
2 large eggs
100ml (3½fl oz) whole milk
Zest of ½–1 small lemon
4 tsp vegetable oil, to cook the pancakes

Lemon and blueberry compote

120g (4oz) fresh or frozen blueberries
20g (¾oz) caster sugar
2 tsp lemon juice

To serve

1 tsp caster sugar
Squeeze of lemon juice
Sour cream

While the pancakes cook, prepare the blueberry compote. Combine the blueberries, sugar and lemon juice in a saucepan and cook over a medium heat, stirring occasionally, for 10–15 minutes, or until the mixture is syrupy.

Once the pancakes are baked, transfer them to plates, spoon some compote into the holes, sprinkle with caster sugar and a squeeze more lemon juice, and serve with a spoonful of sour cream.

Notes

Try some alternative flavours for these pancakes:

Use orange zest instead of lemon and serve the pancakes with chocolate sauce, roasted hazelnuts and a drizzle of cream.

Omit the zest and serve the pancakes with caramelized bananas, caramel sauce and ice cream.

Add a pinch of cinnamon and nutmeg to the batter and serve with apple compote and custard or cream.

Grandma's Egg Custard Tart with Buckwheat Pastry

Grandma Sheila wasn't a big baker; she had a knack for forgetting that things were in the oven, which inevitably meant dishes were on the 'well done' side. Despite this, she was a magician when it came to conjuring up marvellous, simple desserts from a handful of ingredients. A baked egg custard was, without doubt, her signature; wobbly, light as air yet creamy and smooth, and quite literally smothered in grated nutmeg (I hope we all agree this is the only way to enjoy an egg custard). I used to inhale a bowl (or two) when it was served up. Needless to say, it remains my version of pure joy. Here I have refined things a little and baked it as a tart, the nutty buckwheat pastry is the perfect accompaniment to the sweet, aromatic vanilla custard, it tastes as impressive as it looks and can be achieved without too much effort. With a little patience and an ounce of confidence, you can't go wrong!

Serves
8

Hands-on time
25 minutes + 4½ hours resting and chilling time

Cooking time
1 hour 20 minutes

Buckwheat pastry

200g (7oz) plain flour

80g (3oz) icing sugar

¼ tsp baking powder

100g (3½oz) cold unsalted butter, cubed

50g (2oz) egg (about 1 large egg)

30g (1¼oz) buckwheat flour

Custard filling

550ml (20fl oz) whipping cream

1 tsp vanilla extract

95g (3¼oz) egg yolks (from about 5 medium eggs)

50g (2oz) egg (about 1 large egg)

70g (2¾oz) caster sugar

Pinch of sea salt

½ nutmeg

First prepare the pastry. Combine the plain flour, icing sugar and baking powder in a food processor and pulse a few times just to combine. Add the butter and pulse until the mixture resembles fine breadcrumbs, then add the egg and pulse until just clumping together.

Tip in the buckwheat flour and pulse just until the mixture comes together, then tip out onto a large square of cling film and use the cling film to gently flatten the pastry into a disc. Rest the pastry in the fridge for a minimum of 4 hours.

Once rested, roll out the pastry to about 3mm (⅛in) thick and gently transfer to a 20cm (8in) fluted tart tin, pressing the pastry into the sides. Return to the fridge and chill for at least 30 minutes. Preheat the oven to 180°C/160°C fan/350°F/Gas 4.

Line the chilled pastry case with a piece of scrunched up parchment and weigh down with baking beans or uncooked rice. Bake for 15 minutes, before removing the baking beans and parchment and baking for a further 15 minutes until golden. Remove from the oven and allow to cool. Lower the oven temperature to 140°C/120°C fan/275°F/Gas 1.

To make the custard filling, warm the whipping cream and vanilla extract in a saucepan over a low-medium heat, stirring periodically. Meanwhile, combine the egg yolks and egg in a bowl, add the caster sugar and lightly whisk to combine.

Once the cream is steaming, slowly pour it over the egg mixture, tempering at first with a small amount of cream and then gradually streaming in the remainder. Add a pinch of sea salt. Sieve the mixture into to a large jug and spoon off any frothy bubbles.

Place the pastry case onto a baking tray and half fill with the custard mixture, then transfer the tart to the oven shelf and pour in the rest until it just fills the tart case. Grate the nutmeg over the top of the custard.

Bake for 45–50 minutes, or until the custard is set with a light wobble in the centre. Remove from the oven and cool in the tin before serving.

Notes

For a wonderful golden custard, use golden egg yolks.

Don't waste excess pastry:
- Double the filling and bake a second tart or line a muffin tin with rounds cut from the remaining pastry and make mini custard tarts.
- Use this pastry as an alternative for my Forest Fruit Frangipane Tartlets (see page 108).
- Freeze any excess pastry to use at a later date.

If you have a digital thermometer, you can double-check that the custard is baked; when probed, the internal temperature should be 82°C (180°F).

Index

I feel extremely privileged to have been given the opportunity to write this second book and owe a huge amount of thanks to a team of truly wonderful people.

Firstly, thank you to Philippa for your belief and confidence in me from day one and Abi for your support and patience through some of the darker days when I really doubted myself. My gratitude also extends to the whole team at Greenfinch for working so hard to make this book a reality.

A big shout out to Chris, Olimpia and the team at Appetize Food photography... for both putting up with me – you're all saints – but for also producing some incredible photos.

This book would never have been possible without the support of *The Great British Bake Off* family. From the past contestants to all of the Crew, you're the inspiration and reason that I'm here writing this today, Thank you. Thanks also to my little team of cheerleaders out there on social media – I wish I could mention you all by name, but I have some of the most loyal and loving followers and your support means the world to me.

A special thank you to my family, for your love and support throughout, and friends – Harriet, Becca and Rob – you lot deserve a medal. Finally, a massive thank you to my sister, Jess – you're an angel. To my Dad, who passed away in January this year – god I miss you but you got me through some of the harder times. And to Mum, my best friend, my hero and my rock – I love you.

First published in Great Britain in 2022 by

Greenfinch
An imprint of Quercus Editions Ltd
Carmelite House
50 Victoria Embankment
London EC4Y 0DZ

An Hachette UK company

A CIP catalogue record for this book is available from the British Library

HB ISBN 978-1-52942-223-8
eBook ISBN 978-1-52942-224-5

10 9 8 7 6 5 4 3 2 1

Design and layout: Tokiko Morishima
Project editor: Abi Waters
Photography by: Chris Randles/Appetize Food Photography
Food styling: Steph Blackwell
Prop and food styling: Olimpia Davies

Printed and bound in China

Papers used by Greenfinch are from well-managed forests and other responsible sources.